# YOUR
# PUPPY
*Choice and Care*

# YOUR
# PUPPY
## *Choice and Care*

**Written by Catherine Sutton**
**with special research on breeds by Peter Newman**

FOREWORD BY TOM & ANN STEVENSON

**MEREHURST PRESS**
LONDON

This book is dedicated to
Catherine Sutton
who died during its preparation.

Published 1987 by Merehurst Press
5 Great James Street
London WC1N 3DA

ISBN 0 948075 06 6

Edited by Jenny Vaughan
Designed by Roger Daniels
Typeset by AKM Associates (UK) Ltd, Southall, London
Colour separation by Fotographics Ltd, London–Hong Kong
Printed in Spain

## ACKNOWLEDGEMENTS

Adams Picture Library 129 below; Animal Photography 12 left, 14, 16 below, 17 below, 23, 45, 51, 52 above, 57, 59, 74, 77, 80, 81 above, 82, 84, 86, 88, 93, 96, 98, 99, 101, 110, 112, 114, 120, 134, 136, 139 below, 140, 144; Ardea 8, 43, 46, 85 below, 106, 107 above, 108, 115 below, 125; Bruce Coleman Ltd. 35, 78, 117 and back jacket top right; David Dalton 41, 47, 81 below, 109; Barry Day 118 above; Valerie Ferry 10; Mr and Mrs Foreman 92; Marc Henrie 31, 32, 34, 36 and back jacket top left, 42, 48, 49, 50, 71 above, 73, 76, 97, 111, 115 above, 124, 126, 129 above, 135, 137; Miss de Lavis-Trafford 91; Natural History Photographic Agency 9, 67; Diane Pearce 18, 55, 65, 66, 70, 104, 127, 142; Royal Mail 76 below; Russell Fine Art 12 middle and right, 40 below, 83, 113, 131; Spectrum 15, 16 above, 17 above, 22, 24, 33 below, 38, 39, 40 above, 44, 54, 60 both, 61, 62, 63, 64, 71 below, 72 both, 75, 79, 85 above, 87, 89, 95, 100 both, 102, 103, 107 below, 118 below, 119, 123, 128, 132, 138, 139 above, 141 and back jacket bottom right, 143; Tony Stone Photolibrary front jacket, 27, 37, 52 below, 68, 94, 116, 130 both; Mrs C. Wright 33 above; ZEFA 30, 53, 56, 58, 105, 121, 122.

# CONTENTS

# FOREWORD

Catherine Sutton, warmly regarded as the First Lady of Dogdom in Britain, was in fact a citizen of the world, welcomed wherever the fellowship of gentle folk with a caring for animals could be found. She was the ultimate authority on every aspect of the Sport of Dogs: breeder, judge, author, and mover-and-shaker on the road to progress. She never doubted that man and dog were made for each other, or that each has much to give the other in a very special relationship.

In *Your Puppy: Choice and Care*, she produced a book which tells how to make the most of this relationship. It is designed to act as a comprehensive guide in choosing, rearing and training a puppy suitable for your needs; giving invaluable aid to anyone entering into dog ownership with, perhaps, less knowledge than he or she could wish. It offers the opportunity to get the most out of your pet, at home, in the show ring, obedience training, in the field or wherever your interest lies.

It does not neglect the dog as a companion, for this is the whole idea in bringing the new dog into your life. This book will help you to choose which it will be, from over a hundred breeds presented in pictures and described in detail.

With this book, you will share in the help and guidance Mrs Sutton gave so generously to us and to others everywhere, who profited from her expertise in all phases of the dog world.

TOM AND ANN STEVENSON
*Santa Barbara, California*

# A NEW PUPPY

The prospect of getting a new puppy is exciting for everyone in a family, especially the children. However, the excitement should not be allowed to overshadow the importance of thinking seriously about the undertaking. Once your family has a dog, it will require a certain amount of work and a lot of commitment. Remember that, after all, the puppy will not choose you – you will choose the puppy, and it will be up to you to do your best for your new charge.

It is important to decide what you want from a dog, and what you can offer to it. Do you want a guard dog? Do you want something playful and energetic? Do you have room for a large dog?

There are other considerations too. You may be attracted by a breed you knew as a child – but will such a dog be happy with your present life-style? Children especially may be won over by the way a dog looks, but there is a lot more to suitability than this. The most important considerations are practical ones, and these must be thought through as you choose, and before you make, your final decision.

## Size

Irish Wolfhounds and Great Danes are majestic-looking dogs, and they make marvellous companions, but it is impossible to keep such a dog in a tiny flat or a very small cottage. Their wagging tails destroy everything in their way, and these large animals need plenty of space to grow up and play in, quite apart from the demands they will make in terms of regular exercise.

These problems arise in all the larger breeds, and for those with limited space, a smaller type of dog, even one of the toy breeds are a much better choice. They are also best for those on a tight budget, since they tend to cost less to keep. Obviously, the larger a dog is, the more it is likely to eat.

## Noise

It is also important to know that some dogs are much noisier than others. The list of breeds in Part Two will help here. If you live in a crowded area, with other houses nearby, this is something you should take into consideration. A dog that barks whenever it is left alone can put severe strain on relationships between neighbours.

## Grooming and care

Before you buy a puppy, think very carefully about the time you will have to spare to groom it and to keep it looking good. Some breeds need more attention than others, and it is very important to take this into account. It is no good the family deciding on a poodle, an Afghan or an Old English Sheepdog if no one is going to keep its coat in good condition, or pay for this to be done professionally. Such a dog, if neglected, can end up with its coat so badly matted that the only thing to do is take the clippers and remove it completely. No dog in this state can possibly be happy, and allowing this to happen suggests the owner should not really have a dog at all. There are plenty of smooth-coated dogs that need much less attention, and it is best to opt for one of these if you cannot attend to the grooming needs of a long-haired dog.

## Exercise

Exercise is another factor to consider when considering your chosen breed. While your puppy is growing up, it should be able to get all it needs in the garden, but as it grows older it must have more exercise, both free-range and controlled.

The actual amount of exercise depends on the breed, and guidance is given in Part Two. In all cases it is important to make sure the dog does not get bored. A dog that is left alone without much human companionship will find all sorts of ways to occupy its time, including getting into a great deal of mischief. Any bad habits it forms at this time are hard to break – so it is vital to make sure your dog gets its fair share of your time and that exercise and playtime are part of a daily routine. It will pay dividends in the end.

If you are not very agile, or cannot for some reason take the dog for a long walk most days of the week, it is best to settle for a smaller dog. Lack of size does not mean a lack of character. Some of the smaller dogs, including toys, make companions as charming as many of the bigger dogs.

## Training

Some breeds need much more firm handling than others when you first begin training. You must be prepared for this, and it is really best if you have some experience of bringing up one of these breeds. Otherwise, it might be better to select a more easily trained animal.

However, you should not think that a breed that needs firm handling will not be a good companion. It certainly can be – and once trained, no animal could be more devoted to its owner. But if, through your ignorance, the dog is not trained properly, it can become a rogue that will be a worry, and may not be acceptable in society.

## A dog or a bitch?

Having decided on a breed, the next step is to choose between a dog and a bitch. If you are looking simply for companionship, there is much to be said in favour of both sexes. The decision is really up to you. A bitch can present a little inconvenience when she comes into season and she has to be watched carefully, particularly when she is ready to be mated. However, there are now many remedies on the market which can help disguise the situation and if the owner is careful there should be few problems. Those who really feel they cannot cope could make use of one of the many good boarding kennels that are well equipped to deal with the situation.

If your choice of dog depends on size, it is worth remembering that a dog will usually grow to be bigger and will usually be stronger and taller than a bitch. Some people feel that bitches are better with children and more affectionate. Others have found both sexes equally loyal and lovable, with charming characters and always good with the family.

## Two dogs

Few things are more rewarding than a well-trained dog – except perhaps two. They can keep each other company when their owners are out, and they can learn from each other too – though perhaps not always the kinds of things you might hope for. It is amazing how well two dogs can get on with each other, even two of the same sex. (If you choose to keep a dog and a bitch together, though, you will have to deal with the problems of the bitch coming into season. You might be advised to have the bitch spayed, unless you want to breed from her.)

## The family dog

With hundreds of breeds to choose from, quite apart from the infinite variety of cross-breeds, making a decision can be difficult. Generally, it is probably a good idea for a family dog to be a tough, hardy animal with a good steady temperament and no sign of nervousness. A little bit of mischief in its character and a sense of adventure are good signs – though too much of either of these traits will cause problems. Most dogs are faithful to their own family and well-behaved if they are brought up properly, but it is worth taking your time over the choice and selecting carefully.

# WHERE TO FIND YOUR DOG

Choosing a puppy is not simply a matter of deciding on the breed and then going out and buying the first one you see. After all, the dog will be with you for many years and you hope it will give you a great deal of pleasure. Just as you would not buy a car about which you knew nothing from a dealer of whose reputation you were not sure, so you should not buy a dog without careful thought and research. Buy from someone who knows about the dog – not from a pet shop, or even an established store.

### Buying from a breeder

Whether you choose a recognized breed of dog or a more humble cross-bred, try to learn something of its background. This usually means going to a breeder. To find out about local breeders, look in the various weekly or monthly dog publications. You should be able to find these at any good newsagent.

All the really good breeders give plenty of time, care and thought to the puppies that are born in their kennels. They will spend a long time, perhaps years, planning litters and their future breeding programme, always hoping to improve their stock. Such breeders will always sell direct to new owners rather than to an in-between source, as they want to have some idea themselves about what the puppy's new home will be like. They need to approve you, just as you need to approve them.

By buying direct from a breeder, you will get the chance to look at the best stock available. More than that, you will get the chance to see the puppy's dam and probably the sire and other relations.

You will also be able to make up your mind about the conditions in which the puppy you want has been reared. This is a very important point. One glance will be able to tell you whether these look clean, healthy and of the type you would like your puppy to come from. Good conditions, good rearing and a good environment are all important in the early days of a puppy's life and a kennel run by a conscientious breeder will provide these.

Even if you are happy to choose a cross-bred rather than a pedigree, it is still as well to buy from the breeder. It could be seen as even more important, for at least you are able to see the dam and the owner may be able to tell you something about the sire. It is useful to know these details as they are the only way of assessing the ultimate size of the dog, and perhaps even the texture and length the coat will grow to. You will also be able to find out about the mother's temperament.

If you make a point of seeing the puppy and its parents in their home, you will be much more likely to get a healthy, happy dog. It is important to avoid the so-called 'puppy farms', where puppies are not usually bred, but collected from various parts of the country and sold in unhealthy conditions. Disease spreads in this way, and your puppy could easily become very sick indeed after you have bought it and taken it home.

### Visting kennels

If there does not appear to be a breeder of the kind of dog you want in your area, it is worth making the effort to drive some distance to find one. If you plan carefully, and make it a day's outing, you may be able to visit several kennels and see the stock offered.

*But remember . . .*
- Kennel-owners are very busy people and have to stick to a rigid timetable. It is important to make definite arrangements and to be in time for your appointment. Dogs have a very set routine, and it will not be appreciated if you arrive, say, in the middle of feeding time. But if everything is properly arranged, kennel owners are always pleased to show their stock and will be delighted to have a satisfied customer.
- Children will be most welcome, but be careful not to let them dash around the dog runs, exciting and upsetting the dogs.
- Keep a watchful eye to ensure that young children do not poke their fingers through the chain link fencing. They can easily be bitten, which will not help them learn to live with their new pet! Neither will the kennel owner be very pleased.

### Animal sanctuaries

Sadly, a great many owners are irresponsible enough to abandon their dogs when these prove inconvenient or difficult. Such dogs may end up in a sanctuary or 'dog's home', all too often with little chance of a future. We are often counselled to look among these waits for a dog, rather than buying one as a young puppy.

Of course, saving a dog's life by taking it in is a praiseworthy objective, and this should not be underestimated. But if you do decide to take in an abandoned dog, you should be quite clear about the risks you are taking.

These risks centre on the fact that you have absolutely no way of checking up on a dog's background. It may have a very uncertain temperament, especially if it has been ill-treated, and it may prove difficult to live with. You have no means of knowing anything about its parentage and if it is a puppy, this will make it impossible to predict what sort of adult dog it will grow into.

This does not mean that taking in one of these dogs is a bad idea – only that you should weigh up the risks you are taking. It is, however, inadvisable to introduce an adult dog of whom you know nothing, into a family where there are young children.

Finding the right puppy can be an exciting event, and with good planning and care, it can be a happy one too.

**A Beagle with her puppies five days after their birth. It is worth seeing the mother and puppies together to discover how hygienic their living conditions are and assess the mother's temperament.**

# WHAT TO LOOK FOR

If you buy your puppy from a reputable breeder, it is unlikely that you will be sold anything but a healthy, happy, clean dog. After all, the breeder has his or her reputation to consider, and has an interest in making sure that puppies leave the premises in good condition. However, as in buying anything else, it is as well to know what you are looking for, and certainly what to avoid.

**Check before you buy**
Although you should make sure you have a chance to look carefully at the puppies, it is unlikely that the kennel owner will allow you to handle any of them until you have made up your mind which one you want to buy. This is a safeguard against infection – for visitors to kennels can unwittingly carry in germs on clothes, shoes and hands. It is very easy for these to be passed on to any puppy that is handled. At the early stage in its life that you are likely to buy it, it will probably not yet have had all the injections needed to protect it from these infections. A breeder would therefore be very unwise to let a stranger handle the stock. Once you have made your decision, and before you take it from the kennels, you can check it over thoroughly to make sure, as far as you can, that you have a healthy, strong puppy.

*What to look for*
1  There should always be a nice clean smell about young puppies.
2  The eyes should be bright and clear and the nose clean.
3  There should be no irritation of the skin and the coat should gleam with health. (In winter, some puppies may develop a little scurf, which is the result of overheating under a lamp, or even central heating. It should be very slight, and should soon clear up under normal conditions.)
4  Ears should look clean, and should not smell unpleasant. (Do not however, poke into the ears to check on this, as you can damage them. The breeder should check to see that the ears are spotless before handing over the puppy.)
5  Toenails should be cut, and should look tidy. If they are left too long they can be uncomfortable and can eventually spoil the formation of the foot.
6  Ensure that the puppy has been wormed. This should have been done at least twice, if not three times. Almost all puppies have worms, however clean and well managed the kennels. The medicines used for worming today do not upset the puppy, and it is in any case essential

**Puppies' temperaments differ as greatly as do people's, although most will readily make friends. Never choose one that is bad-tempered or aggressive, but a shy puppy may respond to affection.**

if they are to grow well and healthy.
7  In males, two apparently normal testicles should have fully descended into the scrotum by the time the animal is eight weeks old. (Some male puppies, however, are later in developing than others.) If you are buying a male puppy, it must be fully developed in this respect.

**Special points**
Once you have decided on the particular breed, you will soon learn what its special points are. Coat colour for example, is one such point, as well as the shape of the tail, the set of the ears and so on. You should be able to discern all these by the time you buy the puppy, when it should be about eight weeks old.

The mouth and the way the teeth are placed are not so easy to judge at this age, as the baby teeth are still in place. However, unless you are buying a puppy you intend to show, this is not very important, as long as the teeth look clean and healthy and the gums are a nice pink colour.

**Character**
Most puppies are out-going personalities and will readily make friends. You should be wary of a shy one that tends to run away and hide under its bed as it may grow up into a neurotic dog. But do not dismiss it out of hand – there may in fact be nothing wrong temperamentally. Such a puppy may have been badly bullied by its companions, and affectionate human companionship and extra attention may convince it that life is really not so bad, after all. Like humans, some dogs are

more shy than others.

Shyness is vastly less serious than aggressiveness. Never take on a puppy that shows signs of this or bad temper. This is one of the best reasons for buying from a breeder. You will be able to judge from the puppies' dam just what sort of temperament she is likely to pass on, and you may be able to do the same with the stud dog. Temperament is very important when a dog is to be your companion for several years to come, especially if it is be brought up with your children.

**Lastly . . .**
It is very important for a puppy to have a good start in life, and this depends on the way the kennel it comes from is run. You will easily be able to assess this just by looking around and noticing the condition of the dogs. If they look happy, well fed, contented and cared for, you can assume that the puppy has begun life with an advantage. A less fortunate puppy may never catch up. This is especially true of larger breeds where the correct rearing and feeding programmes must be carried out, to ensure that the right bone and substance is achieved.

If you are unsure about anything concerned with the puppy you choose, you should not hesitate to ask the breeder. If you have any worries about the puppy's health, such as a slight cough, a small scratch here or there or simply a little listlessness, be honest with the breeder and say you would prefer not to take the puppy until you are sure that all is well. A good, serious-minded breeder should not see this as a problem.

# BRINGING YOUR PUPPY HOME

The day you bring your puppy home is a very important one in its life, and you will need to give the event some careful thought to make the transition from the kennel to your house as easy as possible.

### Before the puppy arrives
Preparations are important. Before you bring the puppy home you should already have decided where it is to sleep and have the bed ready. You should also have a diet sheet provided by the puppy's breeder, so that you can get in a good supply of the food it will need. Make sure you have all the other equipment necessary – a feeding bowl, a water bowl, the right grooming kit for the breed you have chosen and titbits such as chocolate drops to use as rewards when you are training the dog. Choose a collar and lead as recommended by the breeder, and buy a special toy or two – or you may find your puppy making off with slippers and children's toys.

### Beds and bedrooms
The kind of bed you choose depends very much on the dog you plan to get. Clearly a bed that suits a Rottweiler is hardly suitable for a Yorkshire Terrier. But whatever sort of dog you have chosen, it is inadvisable to buy anything costly until the puppy has got over his teething problems. A basket or bed can be reduced to shreds at this time.

A wire travelling box makes a very good bed for a young puppy – but only for smaller breeds up to, say, the size of a Beagle or Cocker Spaniel. Bigger breeds will quickly need more space than the box provides, for they grow very fast.

The wire box has another advantage apart from being hard to destroy. It is impossible to shut the puppy away for regular rest periods, or when it is important to keep it out of the way. Like any bed, the box should be raised a little above floor level, and kept in a draught-free spot. Many people choose to keep the bed in the kitchen or utility room, where the floor is easy to clean in case of accidents. Puppies that are brought up in a cage soon realize that this is their own area, where they sleep and where their toys are kept. They will quickly learn not to make a mess in the cage, for few puppies like the discomfort this brings. Provided they are given the opportunity to relieve themselves, it is amazing how quickly they will learn to keep their home clean.

When you are ready to buy a permanent bed for your puppy, you will be able to choose from a wide selection of models ranging from the serviceable

**Every dog should have its own bed which should be kept out of any draughts.**

and reasonably priced to the exotic and expensive. The best place to see everything available is at a large dog show, where there will be a number of trade stands, but you could equally well visit any good pet store.

### The day the puppy arrives
It is really best for two people to make the journey to the breeder to pick up the puppy. Otherwise, it will have to be dumped in a box for the journey and there will be no human hands to comfort it. Take a towel to put on your knee, or to wrap the puppy in if the weather is cold. It is also a good idea to take some newspaper, in case it is travel sick. Make sure that you get all the necessary documentation from the breeder, such as Kennel Club registration forms, Veterinary Certificates if the puppy has had any injections, a diet sheet (if you do not have one already) worming details and so on. Follow the advice of the breeder very carefully, especially in respect of diet. The change of conditions will be a traumatic time for the puppy, and it will be better not to add to the problems by changing the diet as well as everything else.

The puppy is bound to be confused when it first arrives in its new home. Be gentle and kind, and give it time to settle in its new surroundings.

### The first few days
Be strict with your puppy right from the start, and do not give in when you hear pathetic little cries in the night. The puppy will soon learn to sleep in its own quarters without any fuss. It will need a great deal of rest and sleep in its early stages, and children may need to be told

this and made to understand that the puppy is not a plaything. They may learn too that pets need care and attention, and that this is a responsibility. If they have agreed to play a part in educating and caring for their dog, they must realize that it should have its basic needs met whether it is wet or fine outside, and however good a programme there is on television. Dogs are creatures of habit, and a regular routine is essential.

### Health
The most common problem puppies develop in their first few days in a new home is an upset stomach. In fact, this should not happen if the diet sheet is followed properly – do not think you are being kind by offering variety in these early days. Be careful, too, not to overfeed.

In winter, keep the puppy at a warm, comfortable and even temperature and apart from making short trips outside, this should ensure there is no danger of catching a chill.

Do not allow the puppy to meet other dogs until it has been fully injected against the various virus infections dogs are prone to. Let the puppy settle in for about a week and then make an appointment with your veterinary surgeon so that you can be advised about injections. There are a variety of opinions about the best age for injections and is best to follow your own veterinary surgeon's advice. It is also a good idea to get to know him or her, and have your puppy checked over.

If possible, try to get the veterinary surgeon to see the puppy at home. A visit to the surgery can be hazardous before the puppy has had all the necessary injections, as a virus infection could easily be passed on actually at the surgery and your puppy could be very sick indeed.

### Exercising your new puppy
While it is still very young, your puppy will get all the exercise it needs in the house and garden. Long walks are not only unnecessary, they can actually be harmful. After all, when a human baby starts to walk, you would hardly think of taking it for a trek across the common. Remember that puppies, like children, need plenty of rest while they are growing. They will also need plenty of food at regular intervals, clean conditions and daily grooming. You should remember too to make sure that there is always a bowl of fresh, clean water available. Use one of the non-spill dishes that are available, as this will ensure that your puppy will not tip water all over the floor.

# TRAINING AND EXERCISE

A well-trained puppy gives great pleasure to the people it lives with and to everyone it meets. It knows its place – and does not rule the household. It is a justifiable source of pride and a reward for all the energy, thought and patience its owners must put into its care and training in the first few weeks.

**Settling down**

A new puppy needs time to settle into its surroundings before any sort of training begins. Allow it to lick the fingers of all the family members, so that it can get accustomed to their individual smells. It will soon realize it is among friends and will quickly become part of the household, forgetting all about its previous life in the kennels.

At eight to ten weeks – which is the age when it will probably join the family – the puppy will have only three objectives in life. Food, of course, is the most important part of its existence. Secondly, it will want to play and have some fun. Thirdly, when it has had enough of the first two, it will want to sleep. You can use the combination of these three things when you train your puppy.

**Basic training**

Basic training should consist of three things:
● the puppy must learn the words 'no' and 'yes',
● it must learn its name and, of course;
● it must learn to be clean in the house.

At the beginning, it is best for only one person in the family to be responsible for training the puppy. This will save the puppy from becoming confused and ensure that the same words and methods are used all the time. Once the puppy has mastered the basic commands, then the rest of the family can use them. It is important, though, that only one person gives a command at any one time, or the poor puppy will become completely perplexed. It will not know who to obey, and will finish off by obeying no-one. Training can be considerably upset if children tease or torment the puppy. This should never be allowed, for the puppy cannot be expected to know what is happening, and will become very confused. Be fair at all times. The puppy will understand this.

**'Yes' and 'no'**

When you are starting to train a puppy, never confuse it with a string of long words. Use the words in a suitable manner to show what you mean. It is no good saying 'no' in a happy, breezy sort of way. When a trainer says 'no,' that is what is meant, and the tone of voice must indicate this every time the word is mentioned. The reverse is also true. When the puppy has been good, indicate this in a quiet, gentle voice and give it a kindly pat. The puppy will soon know from the tone of voice you use whether it has been good or bad or whether it has done right or wrong.

*Teaching the puppy its name*

It is essential to teach the puppy its name. You will probably have selected this even before you bring it home. Try to choose a simple name that rolls of the tongue easily, and use it whenever you want to attract the puppy's attention. It will soon realize that the name is its property and will respond to it quickly. When this happens, do not forget to praise the puppy and it is a good idea to give it a titbit as a reward.

Most dogs want to please their owners, and get great pleasure from doing so. A well-trained dog is a happy dog – a fact that may be encouraging to remember if training is not perhaps progressing as fast as you had hoped!

*Learning to be clean*

Once you have taught your puppy its name, the next essential thing it must learn is to be house clean. This should not present any real problem.

An eight-week-old puppy has very little control over its bladder and bowel movements and needs to relieve itself about a dozen times a day. There is a fairly set pattern to this: immediately after waking, after exercise and after each meal.

Always put it outside to relieve itself as soon as it has finished eating. When this has been done, be quick with your praise. If a puppy is given the opportunity to go outside on all the occasions that it is likely to need to do so, it will soon learn what is required and will begin to trot to the door itself. When this happens, tell it what a good dog it has been and let it outside immediately.

The puppy must have your co-operation at this stage. As soon as it indicates that it wants to go outside, the request must be met immediately, however inconvenient this may be for you. A puppy will usually sniff around in circles to find a place to squat, giving you enough time to put it outside.

Of course, it is easier to housetrain a puppy in summer, when you can leave a door open and the puppy can go in and out as it pleases. In winter, this is usually impossible, and in any case the puppy will not be very enthusiastic about venturing outside. Obviously, any puppy would like to relieve itself indoors in bad weather – but it must be taught that this is not right and should not be accepted.

Newspaper can help at this time of year. Spread it out in a corner of the floor and the puppy will soon realize that this is the place it can relieve itself. If it attempts to do it on the floor, just lift the puppy very gently and put it on the newspaper and, when the puppy has performed there, praise it well. The newspaper can gradually be moved right to the door and eventually be thrown outside. The puppy should understand that this is the place where it must go.

Of course, there are some puppies that are more difficult to train than others, and night-time is often a special problem. One remedy is to shut the puppy up in a box or a cage as described in *Bringing your puppy home*. The puppy will usually try to keep this clean.

The old idea of rubbing the puppy's nose in the offending puddle may possibly have proved effective but there are so many nicer ways of teaching good behaviour, more respectful to your puppy, that this rather crude method should not really be recommended.

Puppy-owners with gardens have, of course, an advantage in house-training their pet, but it is quite easily done in a flat. Use a newspaper, or a box of sawdust – or try the special deodorized 'cat litter' which is widely available. But do not use either litter or sawdust with any breed, such as Pekinese or Shih Tzus, that has vulnerable eyes, as specks may lodge in the eyes and cause ulceration.

**Punishment**

Occasionally you may have to scold your puppy, but it is important to remember that in training, rewarding a puppy for what it does well will prove far more effective than punishing it for a poor performance. You should only punish a puppy to show severe displeasure. Too much punishment may lead to the puppy maturing into a maladjusted adult: either very aggressive or far too submissive and easily intimidated. Both of these traits are difficult to correct and any further training will be useless.

It is never wise to scold a puppy or dog unless you have caught it in the act of doing something wrong and it is quite clearly the guilty party. Never hit a dog with your hand. Apart from the pain it might cause, remember that the dog knows your hand as something that pets, pats and provides food. Suddenly turning round and using the same kind hand to punish the dog can make it very wary and reluctant to come too close. A rolled-up newspaper is a very effective weapon and a gentle hit on the puppy's backside will make it understand very quickly that what it has done is wrong. Your tone of voice too will tell the puppy whether what it has done is right or not and in the early stages at least, there should be no need to resort to the rolled-up newspaper.

### Short lessons

The basic training described here is very important. As it must start at an early age, it is advisable that, until the puppy is well established as a member of the household, it is only given this simple, elementary training. This should not be very tiring, and each lesson should be kept short, so that the puppy does not become bored or distracted.

### Training with a collar and lead

When the puppy has learned how to be clean in the house, to recognize its own name and understand 'yes' and 'no', it will be well on the way to mastering further obedience training.

### *The collar*

A puppy should be taught from an early age to wear a collar. It can start at eight weeks old, wearing the collar for a short period each day. Make sure you are always nearby when the puppy is wearing the collar. If it is unhappy with it and tries to get it off, it may get it caught round something. When this happens, and the puppy twists and turns, the results can be tragic.

For the same reason, you should never use a choke (or 'check') chain on a young puppy. Its name alone suggests why not. These chains are excellent for training purposes, but should never be left on any dog, and should certainly not take the place of an ordinary leather collar. If you are using one of these chains, it is important that the large ring should be at the side of the dog's neck, thus allowing the chain to run freely.

Placing a choke chain on a French Bulldog. The chain's large ring must remain at the side of the neck to allow the chain to move freely.

Most puppies take to the collar with no trouble at all, particularly if they are trained from an early age. When the puppy comes to you, gently slip a lightweight collar around its neck, pat the puppy and praise it, giving it confidence by talking to it. If you work this way, it will soon forget it has a collar on. Repeat this once or twice a day and when the puppy seems to pay no attention to the collar, you can start work with a light lead.

It is a good idea to have the dog's name and address engraved on a disc and attached to the collar. The dog must wear the collar at all times when it is out on the road or public highway. This is required by law in most countries.

### *The lead*

Some puppies resent a lead to start with and behave like bucking broncos. You should pay no attention to this. Talk to the puppy kindly and always praise it if it goes even a little way with the lead.

This exercise should never be treated as a game, and if the puppy attempts to grasp hold of the lead, it must be told at once that this is not right, and scolded for it. Do not allow this habit to take hold, for it is very difficult to cure.

A puppy that simply digs its heels in and refused to move, giving you a withering look as it does so, is more difficult to cope with. You will need a lot of patience. Talk to this puppy very gently and try to persuade it that life with a collar and lead is not as bad as it seems.

Only one handler should ever try to get the puppy lead-trained. If you let the whole family have a go you will only confuse the animal. Once the training is complete, though, everyone can have a turn at taking the dog out on the lead.

### *Walking to heel*

The next step is to teach the puppy to walk to heel on the lead. This can be done using either a slip-lead or a choke chain and lead.

With the puppy on your left-hand side, give the command 'Heel!', and walk straight on. Having had some experience of a collar and lead, it should respond to the walk-to-heel exercise quite quickly. If the puppy pulls away from you, jerk it back by using the command 'Heel!' or 'Heel!' plus its name. The minute you feel it is alongside you, let the lead slacken. When you have done this once or twice, the puppy will soon realize that if it runs on or lags behind, it will get a nasty jerk in the neck,

Of course, every dog wants to investigate the lovely smells it finds on

**Every dog should be trained to walk to heel both for its safety and yours.**

its walks, but it must be patient and wait until it is well enough trained to be let off the lead. This is especially important when it meets other dogs.

### 'Sit'

Next we come to the very important 'sit' exercise. A puppy can be taught to recognize the word 'sit' and obey it from as early as twelve weeks.

It is important to make sure a puppy learns to sit in the proper position – looking alert and attractive with its back straight. Take the puppy to a quiet place where it can concentrate and, if possible, somewhere where it can sit with its back to a wall. Press your hands down gently on the hips and at the same time tell the puppy to 'sit'. Keep pressing down until it understands what you want. When it does, do not forget to praise it. These lessons should not be too long to start with, as the puppy will

**A dog should look alert even when sitting, and should be completely attentive to its owner.**

get bored and want to dash off and find something more exciting to do.

When it has mastered the 'sit' command, take the puppy away from its own surroundings to some public place and make it put into practice what it has learned at home. If your training has been properly done, it will have no problem about obeying you – in spite of the many distractions around.

### 'Sit and come'

'Sit and come' is the next step. Attach some rope to the end of the puppy's lead and, having said 'sit,' back away slowly for about two or three yards. If it attempts to move, shout 'Sit!' in a very firm voice. At this stage you must concentrate on the puppy and look at it with steady eyes.

Next, call 'Come!' and with your right hand, signal to the puppy to come. Pull gently on the rope with your left hand. Do not tug, or pull abruptly, and remember to give lots of praise when it is clear that you have been understood and obeyed. Make the puppy 'sit' in front of you, and it will probably look up at you with pleasure in its eyes.

Repeat this exercise once or twice, but do not overdo it at this stage. In a couple of days, lengthen the rope and keep doing this each day until you can successfully complete the exercise from quite a long distance.

The next step comes when you slip the lead off and walk away from the puppy, knowing it will stay put until you give the command. When you turn round, call 'Come!', and give the same indication as before with your right hand. The puppy should immediately come straight to you and sit in front of you.

Dogs usually love this exercise, but whether it is successful or not depends on you. Never be impatient, or worse still, lose your temper. If the dog loses faith in you, you will have to make a great effort to restore it and you will find yourself almost back at the beginning of the training.

### 'Heel free'

The next exercise is 'heel free'. Make the puppy sit on your left side and then slip off the lead. With the word 'heel', you should both walk ahead. You can use your left hand to encourage the dog, patting your own thigh and, if the dog wants to, let it put its nose against your hand. This gives it confidence to stay with you. Talk to it, encouraging it to come along. If it strays, command it to come back to heel immediately, and praise it for doing so.

This exercise should, of course, be practised first in a quiet area and not in a busy place where the dog's attention can easily be distracted and could wander off, perhaps causing an accident.

All this is very good training for dogs that are taken to the show ring, and those that are made to do more advanced work, such as police dogs, guide dogs for the blind and so on.

### Crossing the road

In traffic, your dog should never leave your side. When you want to cross a road, make the dog sit and remain at your side until you are sure that the way is clear. Then command the dog to 'heel' and set of. This will, of course be done while it is on a lead, and after you have repeated this many times, the dog will sit and wait for you instinctively, without waiting for any commands from you.

### Retrieving

Throughout their training, puppies should always have a chance to play. Most of them love to retrieve, and this game can also be used as part of the training – especially in the case of gun-dogs.

Start when the puppy is about twelve weeks old, and choose a soft article to begin with. If there is not much interest, wait until the dog is a little older.

Throw the article a little way and tell the puppy to 'Fetch it!'. It will usually dive towards whatever you have thrown and pick it up. When you give the command 'Fetch it!', encourage the puppy to bring the article all the way back to you. It may decided not to do this – so you will have to be patient as you try to persuade it to bring it back.

When the puppy does bring the article back, give lots of praise and, when it releases the object, reward it with a small titbit. When this exercise is done well, teach the puppy to come back and sit in front of you until you take the article from its mouth. Having accomplished this, it can then be taught to go round you and finish up sitting at your left hand side.

All this takes patience, and the puppy should not be rushed, or given too much to do at one time.

If you feel that your puppy has an aptitude for this work, you could consider going on to more advanced obedience training. The Kennel Club can provide details of Obedience Clubs you could contact.

### A well-trained dog

*Coming when called*
No dog should ever be allowed to think that it can greet other dogs whenever it wants to. A tendency to do this should be stopped immediately. Apart from the danger of picking up infections, a dog will not think of traffic and other dangers as it dashes off to meet another dog. Your dog should always come when you call. If you want to let it off the lead in a park or on a common, you must be absolutely certain that it will not chase sheep, cattle, poultry, or horses and their riders. A dog that chases livestock is liable to be shot on sight, and you will have no legal redress.

*Cars and bicycles*
Chasing cars and bicycles is another habit that should be stopped right at the beginning. If your dog persists in doing this you will have no alternative but to keep it on a lead at all times. The dangers involved in chasing vehicles are, of course, very serious, as the dog could easily cause an accident. Dogs usually take up this habit because they are bored. It should not happen if they are properly cared for and exercised.

*Furniture*
A dog's place is on the floor – not on the furniture. Never lift your puppy on to your knee to talk to it, especially not if it is one of the larger breeds. Bend down to make a fuss of it, but never encourage it to jump up on to your chairs. Otherwise, you may well find one day that your wet and dirty dog has come in from a walk and decided that the best way to get dry is to roll on the settee. If it has always been allowed on the furniture, you can hardly blame the dog if it behaves in this way.

*Barking*
A dog that barks is a nuisance, and can cause problems between neighbours. As with all bad habits, it should be stopped straight away. A dog should be trained from an early age that its job is to bark only when strangers arrive, and to stop as soon as it is told to do so. If the owner is usually with the dog when it barks, training it to stop should not be difficult. A much more serious problem is when the dog is left alone in the house and barks incessantly.

The best way of dealing with this is to put the dog alone in a room and to go away. As soon as it starts to bark, go back and say 'No! No! No!'. Then go off and leave it again. If it still persists in barking, go back and be very cross. Chastise the dog with a rolled-up newspaper and, once again, say very firmly: 'No! No! No!'.

You may have to repeat this once or twice before the dog learns to stop barking. If it is quiet for a period, go back and praise it, even giving it a titbit as a reward to reinforce the message.

*The right pace*
Never try to gallop ahead with your puppy's training. Make sure it really understands its previous lessons before you go on to the next. If things do not seem to be going quite right, stop and ask yourself if perhaps you are the one at fault. Don't simply blame the puppy if it seems badly behaved and disobedient.

## Problem dogs
Of course, there are always a few rogue dogs who simply will not be trained. These can be found in every breed. If it seems that you are unlucky enough to have such a dog, do not be discouraged. Give the dog every chance. Take it to training classes and seek advice from responsible breeders.

Sadly, if all else fails, the only answer is to have the dog put down. It is unwise and irresponsible to pass the dog on to another home unless you are very sure that corrective training will be given by experienced handlers, and that there is hope that, under different conditions, the dog will settle.

## Exercise
All breeds of dogs are naturally very active, and need a certain amount of exercise to keep them fit and happy and to prevent them from becoming bored. However, dogs vary enormously in the amount of exercise they need. Two dogs may have quite different needs even if they are of the same breed – or from the same litter. Small dogs, of course, tend to need less than large ones, while toys may need no more than the chance to run about the house. (However, they appreciate the chance to have the occasional look at the outside world.)

A house dog should have two good walks a day as a rule – but the breeder from whom you get it can advise you about just how much exercise your dog needs as a puppy and as an adult. Many dogs, particularly among the larger breeds, are over exercised as puppies, and this can only harm them.

In any case, it is not a good policy to overdo walks at the beginning of a dog's life, if you do not intend to keep up this routine. The dog will learn to look forward to going out and if the exercise tends to get less and less, it will become bored, unhappy and, almost inevitably, naughty.

Remember that if your dog gets very wet while taking exercise, it must be thoroughly dried when it gets home. If you neglect the dog in this respect, it can result in great discomfort, and a tendency to be rheumatic in later life.

**A child can be responsible for teaching a puppy some simple tricks to their mutual enjoyment.**

## Dogs with children
Bringing up puppies and children together is an education for both parties. The puppy learns to be part of the family, and to fit in with both domestic arrangements and with the children. The children quickly learn that the puppy is not a toy, but a companion. It is alive, and has feelings of its own, which it can share with humans. It should have its own toys and should not be allowed to steal those of the children. Likewise, children should not be allowed to take away the puppy's toys.

Children and puppies alike must rest sometimes, and both should learn to respect this need in each other. Children should not get into the habit of lifting the puppy. They should only do this if it has been hurt and needs to be taken somewhere where it can be given the right sort of attention. They should not tease the puppy, as this teaches it to snap and become bad tempered. At the same time, the puppy should be taught not to bite the children or anybody else for that matter, unless there is a very good reason.

If a puppy starts to growl at the family, it should be chastised straight away, so that it knows it is wrong. A puppy that is allowed to growl will turn into a bad-tempered dog that no one will be able to control, and the only solution to the problem of a bad-tempered dog is to have it put down. But with good handling and proper training, this should never be necessary.

Once the puppy has settled with the family, there is no reason why the children should not take part in its training. Some children have an especially good understanding of animals and this can be reciprocated by the dog.

Children should use the training methods the dog is used to, and should have the same patience that the adult trainer has shown. They could teach a few simple tricks, such as teaching the puppy to give its paw to be 'shaken' on command.

Bringing up children with a dog can be very rewarding, and if it is done properly, they will learn and benefit from each other and be good and loyal friends all the dog's life.

## Dogs in cars

*Car sickness*
Most dogs love travelling in cars. Once your puppy has had all the injections it needs, take it with you whenever you can so that it gets used to car journeys as quickly as possible. Start with short journeys until the puppy is quite a seasoned traveller. If it tends to dribble and look unhappy, you could try one of the safe tablets available to help get over this problem. Very few dogs are bad travellers in cars and it is really a matter of patience and allowing the puppy to get over its initial qualms. Once it realizes that a car journey usually ends in a walk it will soon feel better and will find the whole exercise something it looks forward to.

If your dog seems unable to get over car sickness, you should consult your veterinary surgeon, as there are several stronger antidotes that could be prescribed.

*Some precautions*
1 **Never** leave your puppy alone in a car until you are quite sure it will not get bored while it is on its own and start to tear the inside of the car to pieces. It is surprising how much damage it can do in a short time. If you think the dog will often have to be left alone in the car, it is probably a good idea to buy it a cage or a box so that it can be left in safety. Show dogs usually travel this way are usually happy to jump into the cage, ready for the journey.
2 **Never** leave your dog in the car, even with the windows open, on a hot day. The inside of the car becomes like an oven, and the dog will become extremely distressed. Many dogs have died as a result of this thoughtlessness on the part of their owners.
3 **Do not** allow your dog to stick its head out of the window while the car is travelling. Apart from the fact that this can cause accidents, it is very bad for the dog's eyes and can cause considerable and quite unnecessary problems.
4 **Never** allow your dog to be a nuisance to the driver of the car. At no time should it be permitted to lean over the driver while the car is in motion.

# EQUIPMENT AND GROOMING

Grooming is important whatever breed of dog you have. It should be done regularly, but short-coated dogs are of course much easier to look after than long-coated ones.

Dogs that are kept indoors in air-conditioned houses tend to shed their hair fairly constantly all year, but there is always an increase at the time when they would normally be shedding their coat. It is essential to get rid of the dead coat, otherwise it will irritate the skin, making the dog uncomfortable, or even short-tempered.

Grooming also helps stimulate the sebaceous glands, that provide the oil that keeps the skin in good condition.

**Ready for grooming**
Train your puppy from the beginning to stand quietly, so that you can go over its coat gently with a brush or grooming glove. If it is one of the smaller breeds, such as one of the toys, or a cocker or a beagle, you can put it on a table to groom it. It will soon learn that when it is put there it is going to have some attention of one kind or another. It is a very good idea to get the puppy used to standing on a table, as it will have to do this when it visits the veterinary surgeon. Many show dogs are judged on tables, which means that for them, this training is essential.

**Equipment**
Two different types of brushes and the sort of comb you may need for grooming your dog are shown here. Clippers are not included, but if you want to use them, there is a wide selection available from good pet stores or the trade stands at dog shows. The standholders will have wide experience of the different types of coat among dogs, and will be able to advise you about the best equipment for your needs.

Never economize on cheap scissors if you need them in your grooming kit. Buy the best you can afford, both for barbering and for thinning the coat. If you take care of them, they should last for many years.

Any other items of equipment you need can usually be bought at dog shows if you find them difficult to get hold of in local shops.

It may be worth knowing that if you are going to show your dog, grooming may involve more work than in the case of a family pet. Show trimming and stripping is more complicated as, for example you may have to trim and strip instead of using clippers. In terriers, for example, clippers will destroy the coarse texture of the coat, which is essential for showing. Instead, you will have to hand-strip the coat, which means plucking hair out with your fingers and thumb, or with the aid of a stripping knife.

*Combs*
The best all-purpose comb is one with medium teeth on one side and fine teeth on the other. Use the medium side to tease out the mats and tangles. Do this very carefully, so as not to cause discomfort to the dog. If, for some reason, the coat has become heavily matted or something is tangled up in it, then you should use a large matting comb. This is a heavy, coarse comb, strong enough to bring out the mats and tangles.

**Short-coated dogs**
The amount of grooming a dog needs depends, of course on its coat. Short-coated dogs are, of course, the easiest to deal with and it is usually enough to groom one of these every other day, except when its coat is really coming out. All such a dog needs is for a good hard brush or rubber glove to be taken over the coat. If you want to give it extra polish, then an ordinary shammy leather can be used to give it a shine. Dogs with thicker coats need a strong wire pad with a handle attached to it.

As this goes through the coat, it gathers up old hairs and, at the same time, stimulates the sebaceous glands. The wire teeth of such a pad should not be too harsh or too soft, and the pad should have a foam backing.

**Long-haired dogs – brushing out**
Before you begin brushing, use your hands to feel for tangles, and comb them out. Once this has been done, you are ready to begin.

When brushing out a long-haired dog, it is best to start with the dog's hindquarters and work forwards. This prevents the dog from actually seeing what is happening, and by the time you get to the front, it will have become used to it. Brush with one hand and hold the coat with the other. This will give the dog a feeling of confidence. If you groom your dog on a table with a slippery surface, make it stand on a mat. If the dog slides about during grooming, it will become very uneasy about the whole operation.

Begin by brushing one rear leg and then the other. Move the brush up and then down, in short, fast strokes, making sure that you get under the topcoat, right down to the undercoat. From the rear legs, progress to the front

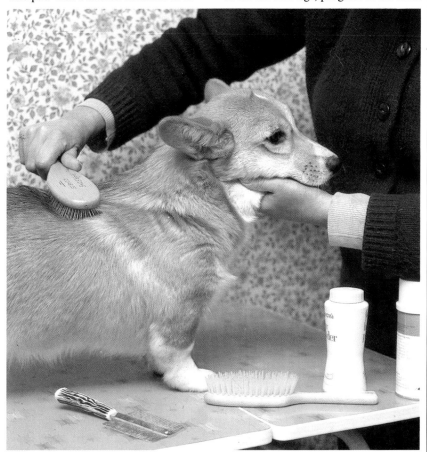

**A short-coated breed such as this Corgi will need only a little grooming.**

ones, and then on to the body coat. Remember to groom under the body, as this area is often neglected and can quickly get matted if it is not groomed.

It is always very important to keep a long-haired dog thoroughly brushed. You can only be sure that you have done the job properly when you can run a comb through the hair without any difficulty.

**Bathing**

Before bathing a dog – especially if it is one of the thick-coated ones, such as a Poodle, an Afghan or a Cocker – it is essential to groom it carefully and make sure all the mats are removed. These will not disappear when bathing: in fact they will become even more tangled, eventually making more work for you – not to mention discomfort to the dog.

*What you need*

Before bathing your dog, make sure that you have everything you need close at hand before you put the animal in the bath. If you do not, and you have to leave it even for a second, you will have a wet dog running all over the house.

**Begin grooming a long-haired dog such as this Rough Collie by first combing out any tangled hair. Every dog should be taught to sit quietly throughout this process while still a puppy.**

Precisely how you bathe your dog will depend on its size and coat. Do it in the open if possible

You will probably need the following:

- **a waterproof apron** for yourself – for obvious reasons;
- **shampoo**. Do not use ordinary household soap, or shampoo designed for humans, which will be too strong for the dog's skin. Choose a dog shampoo, of which there are plenty on the market;
- **a towel**;
- **some cotton wool**, if your dog has sensitive ears. You should use this to plug them gently, to prevent any water getting in;
- **a hair-dryer**, especially if it is a long-coated dog.

*Steps in bathing*

1 Prepare the bath before you introduce the dog to it. The water should be warm, but not too hot.
2 Put the dog in the water and pour water over it with a jug, or use a fine shower. Take care not to get any water in the dog's eyes, either now or, especially not later, when you are using the shampoo.
3 When you have the dog completely soaked right through the hair, rub soap or shampoo thoroughly into its coat. Pay particular attention to its rectum, making sure that it is clean. Use your hands to work up a good lather all over the body, gently talking to the dog as you do so.
4 After this, get rid of the soap. This must be done very thoroughly, so that no trace is left. Use either a jug or a shower; with longer-haired dogs you could even use both. The shower gets right down to the roots of the hair, while the jug will help get rid of the more stubborn suds. Here, as with most aspects of grooming, short-haired dogs are much easier to deal with than long-haired ones.
5 When you have rinsed the dog, squeeze all the excess water from the legs, tail, underparts of the body, the top of the body, the ears and so on. Be careful at this stage, as the dog will realize that it is almost time to get out of the bath, and it will be eager to get out of the water and have a good shake.
6 Now rub the dog briskly with a towel and finish off the process with a hair dryer. In summer, when the weather is fine, there is no reason why it should not be let out into the sunshine to dry off. Take care, though, that when you are not looking, the dog does not go off and find something unpleasant to roll in.
7 Before the dog is quite dry, it is a good idea to brush and trim the coat, so that it lies the way you want it to.

**A few more grooming tasks**

*Ears*

Ears must always be treated very gently, but they should not be ignored. Any excessive hair inside them should be plucked free. The best way of doing this is to rub the hair with some hard chalk, which you should be able to get from any good pet suppliers. The chalk makes the hair hard and brittle, and therefore easier for you to pull out with your finger and thumb, in single, quick motion. This should only take a few minutes to do, but you should make sure you do not leave any chalk in the ear.

To see that the ears are clean, gently insert a piece of cotton wool into the ear and take away any visible dirt. Never prod into the ear, but make sure the ends of the ears are quite clean and that no food is still sticking to them.

If your dog is constantly scratching its ears or shaking its head and is in obvious discomfort, then you should seek advice from a veterinary surgeon. Ears are very tender and delicate, and no unqualified person should interfere with them.

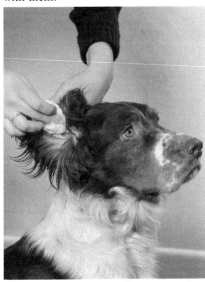

**Clean your dog's ears with cotton wool but never poke anything into them.**

*Nails*

You will have to look after the dog's nails while it is still a puppy, but once it has begun to be exercised on hard surfaces you will probably not have to do anything to control their length. There are several types of nail clippers available, but the guillotine type is the easiest to use. Be careful not to cut the quick (which is easy to see) as this can be very painful to the dog.

If the dew claws have not been removed from a puppy, you should check regularly that they are not

**Clipping a Dalmatian's nails. Regular exercise by itself will normally keep a dog's nails short, but if it is necessary to trim them make sure that the quick is not cut into.**

growing right round and digging into the dog's leg. They should really have been removed at three or four days old, as they serve the dog no useful purpose and can be a great nuisance to the dog. They can catch on everything, including people's clothes, and when torn, they are painful and bleed excessively.

*Teeth*

Teeth should be inspected regularly. Sometimes, a puppy needs help in removing its first teeth, particularly the eye teeth. If they do not drop out easily, the second teeth may grow up out of line and, in a show dog, this would be a disaster. If this problem seems to be occurring, ask your veterinary surgeon to help remove the baby teeth.

As your dog gets older, it may collect tartar around its teeth. If this happens, the teeth should be scaled periodically, whenever it is necessary. However, if the dog has always had hard biscuits and a marrow bone to chew, it should not be bothered with excessive tartar until it is quite old.

*Parasites*

If you groom your dog regularly, you should be able to notice straight away if there are any parasites (fleas or lice) on the skin. Dogs easily collect these when they are out on walks, exploring in the undergrowth and grass. There is no need to worry, but it is best to get rid of them straight away. There are plenty of preparations on the market to deal with them – but remember to check the dog's bedding to see if this is infected, and deal with it straight away.

It is important to act quickly, before the dog has taken to scratching so much that it damages its skin.

# AILMENTS AND HEALTH HAZARDS

Dogs are usually very healthy animals, and a properly and conscientiously cared for dog will be fit and well for most of its life.

However, there a number of things that can go wrong – though many will probably be very minor. For example, a dog may on occasion suffer from a bout of vomiting and diarrhoea. This will usually be short-lived and the body's natural defences should be able to overcome this in a day or two. (If sickness and diarrhoea continue, they could indicate a more serious ailment, perhaps a virus infection, and you should consult a veterinary surgeon.)

## Taking the dog's temperature

If you are at all worried about your dog's health, take its temperature. This should be 38.6°C (101.5°F), though this can vary slightly among individual animals, and tends to be higher during the day and after exercise.

A dog's temperature should be taken with a blunt-ended clinical thermometer, the end of which is smeared with petroleum jelly. Shake the thermometer so that it registers a low reading before you use it – otherwise it may give you an inaccurate result, causing you undue alarm. Insert the thermometer very carefully into the dog's rectum, and keep it there for about two or three minutes, or as stated on the instrument itself or in the instructions that come with it.

Never force the thermometer into the rectum: it should slide in easily and comfortably. After you have withdrawn it, hold it horizontally and twist it around until the reading is clear. Then wipe the thermometer clean, using cotton wool that has been soaked in surgical spirit, and put it back in its case, ready for the next time.

It is worth worrying about both high and low temperatures, and you should contact your veterinary surgeon without delay in either case.

## Medication

If you have to give your dog medicine, you may find it is a good idea to have someone else to help you. One person should hold the dog steady, while the other administers the medicine. Make the dog stand or sit in front of you and, with the fingers of your left hand, pull down the right-hand corner of the bottom lip. Gently pour the medicine into the mouth. Never open the mouth and try to throw liquid into the back of the throat. This can easily make the dog choke or vomit, which will result in all the medicine being lost. Handle the dog gently and try to persuade it to take the medicine.

*A pen or pencil can be used to tighten a tourniquet in an emergency, but never leave it tight for more than fifteen minutes at a time and take the dog to a Veterinary Surgeon at once.*

You will need to adopt a similar approach if the dog has to take a pill. Talk to the dog gently all the time as you open its mouth, and quickly pop the pill on to the back of the tongue. Shut the mouth straight away and, keeping the head high, very gently stroke the throat until the dog swallows. This should mean that the pill is swallowed too – but not always. Some dogs get quite adept at pushing a pill into a corner of their mouth, so that even after they have swallowed, it is still there. Check to see that the pill has actually gone down and then, of course, praise the dog for being so good.

If your dog is difficult about taking pills, try putting one on a favourite titbit, such as a piece of meat or cheese. This can save a lot of fuss, for both the dog and the owner.

## Care of a sick dog

A sick dog should be kept spotlessly clean. It should be given a warm, quiet place to lie and any treatment the veterinary surgeon prescribes should be given regularly and with great patience. All this will help the dog recover much faster.

## Injections

### Basic inoculations

It is very important that your puppy should be injected against distemper, hard-pad, leptospirosis, hepatitis, parvo virus and, in many countries, rabies. If you intend to make use of boarding kennels at any time, you should also make sure your dog is protected against kennel cough. Booster doses for these various infections should be given annually.

## Common ailments

### Abrasions

Dogs are active animals, and are bound to get a few scars and injuries now and again. If this happens, clean the wound thoroughly, dry it with cotton wool and apply zinc or calamine ointment. You may need to use a bandage to prevent the dog licking the wound, but this can cause extra problems. Most dogs are irritated by the bandage and spend a lot of time trying to tear it off. The only solution may be to make a hood from a plastic bucket, which makes it impossible for the dog to reach the wound. Cut the bottom out of a plastic bucket, and make holes around the base of the sides. Using these holes, thread the bucket on to a collar with string. With its head in this hood, the dog cannot get at the wound and, although it may look uncomfortable, the injury will heal much faster.

Making a hood is much more effective than muzzling the dog, as the dog may tend to rub the muzzle on the sore place and make it even worse.

Serious cuts and wounds should be dealt with as soon as possible by a veterinary surgeon.

## Accidents

If your dog is unfortunate enough to be involved in a road accident, keep it absolutely quiet and call your veterinary surgeon. Do not give any stimulants, such as brandy, if there is an external haemorrhage, or if there may be an internal one.

If your dog has cut its foot badly, perhaps by treading on a piece of broken glass, bandage the wound as tightly as possible to stop the bleeding and apply a tourniquet somewhere between the wound and the heart. To tighten the tourniquet, push a pencil or something similar through the bandage and twist it. Do not leave a tourniquet on for more than fifteen minutes at a time.

*Note*: Take care with this, as the dog is under great stress and is liable to bite you. It is a good idea to tape its mouth with a bandage or a stocking before you try to treat the wound. Put the tape around the dog's mouth a couple of times, then bring it under the throat, cross it and bring it up on to the neck, where you should tie it very firmly.

## Anal glands – infection

The anal glands are situated on each side of the anal opening, and if they become infected they cause the dog great discomfort. The complaint is most common in toy dogs, rather than bigger ones, and with correct diet and where the motions are solid, anal glands should not give any trouble.

If they do become infected, the dog will keep turning round to lick itself and even drag its bottom along the floor in an attempt to get rid of the discomfort. A slight discharge and an unpleasant smell will indicate that the glands are badly affected.

Take the dog to your veterinary surgeon, who can squeeze the glands and get rid of their contents. If this is done straight away, it will prevent abcesses forming, and these can be very painful to the dog.

## Arthritis

Arthritis is an inflammation or disease of a joint. It is usually found in older dogs. The joint becomes swollen and is painful to the touch. It can make a dog quite lame. Rest and warmth are essential, and if the pain seems very bad your veterinary surgeon may prescribe gentle painkillers.

## Bites

If your dog is bitten by another animal, clean the wound and apply penicillin ointment or iodine regularly, until all discharge stops. After that, apply a healing ointment. If the wound is deep, take the dog to a veterinary surgeon who will not only treat the wound but will also give the dog an injection to help prevent any infection.

## Burns and scalds

Burns and scalds should not be treated at home unless they are very minor. A dog may suffer from shock however slight an accident may seem to be.

Clean the burn and remove any dirt, straw, food or other foreign matter that might be sticking to it. Douse the burn with cold water for 10–15 minutes. Do not apply any ointments. Take the dog to a veterinary surgeon at once.

## Colic

Colic is an acute pain in the abdomen, which is usually caused by indigestion, flatulence or constipation, all of which are often the result of incorrect feeding. The pain does not usually last long, but it upsets the dog and makes it restless. It may even whine and cry out. Relief comes when the bowels are evacuated.

There are three simple precautions you can take to avoid colic:
- **never** give your dog a heavy meal late at night;
- **never** feed it with unsoaked biscuit meal;
- **never** feed it with food that is too wet.

## Constipation

Constipation is usually caused by a badly balanced diet. The dog finds it difficult to pass its stools, which will be very hard and dry. Try a change of diet and check whether the dog is getting enough exercise. If diet does not ease the problem, then give a laxative such as liquid paraffin, Milk of Magnesia or Epsom salts in small doses over a period of time.

## Coprophagy

'Coprophagy' is the name given to a condition that happens only occasionally, where the dog eats its own faeces. One theory is that it is caused by a vitamin deficiency, another is that it indicates an iron deficiency. A simple way to deal with it is to remove the cause of trouble, making sure that there are no faeces left lying around and so no chance of the dog finding them. Most dogs will eat the faeces of cows and horses if they are given the chance.

## Dandruff

Dandruff, in dogs and humans, is a scurfy condition of the skin and hair. A good grooming once or twice a day with a stiff brush or a hound glove will increase the circulation, stimulate its nerves and generally improve the condition. As with other problems, dandruff can be caused by bad diet and lack of exercise.

## Diarrhoea

Diarrhoea is often caused by worms in puppies, but can also be the result of a change in the diet, or improper feeding. If worms are not the cause, and the diarrhoea persists, consult a veterinary surgeon, as the condition could be the beginning of a more serious ailment.

## Distemper

Distemper is a highly infectious disease and a dog owner is really failing in his or her responsibilities if the dog is not inoculated against it. Canine distemper is caused by a virus which invades the nervous system. This results in fits, chorea and even paralysis, and the disease is seldom cured. The dog will have a high temperature, and will appear completely out of sorts. There will be a discharge from the nose, and probably a cough as well. Loss of appetite and listlessness will follow. The eyes will seem weak and very sensitive to light, and there will be a discharge from them.

*Note:* If your dog appears to have distemper, do not take it to the veterinary surgeon, as this will spread the disease. Ask for a home visit.

If your dog is to have any hope of recovering from this disease, it will need very patient and dedicated nursing, day and night. It is much better, of course, to make sure the dog has all the inoculations it needs in the first place.

## Ears – infections

Bad ears are usually neglected ears, and serious problems such as ulceration do not happen overnight.

People tend to use the term 'canker' very loosely, to describe any irritation of the ears. It is a condition that is more common in long-haired dogs and is caused by tiny parasites which get into the canal of the ear and multiply rapidly. There are two forms, wet and dry, and both should be treated at once. If you notice your dog scratching its ears, look inside to see what the problem is. If you find a dark, unpleasant-smelling substance there, you can be sure it is canker. If this is allowed to persist, the condition will become chronic and can only be cured by means of an operation. It is a good idea to make a regular habit of checking the ears whenever the dog is being groomed, but never poke into the ear with any sort of instrument. Ears are very sensitive and you can damage them badly. It is best to seek veterinary advice.

### Eczema

Eczema is a non-contagious skin disease that many experts believe is caused by diet. It may also be a nervous condition. The skin is irritable, which make the dog scratch continually, licking and nibbling itself all the time. This of course makes things worse. The affected parts become red and sore-looking and produce a sticky discharge.

Cut all the hair away from the sticky area and apply benzyl benzoate. You may also have to make the dog wear a bucket hood, to stop it reaching the eczema (see under *Abrasions*).

### Entropion

Entropion is a condition in which the eyelids are inverted, and is more common in some breeds than in others. Look for it in a puppy that has rather weepy eyes. If you examine it closely you may find that the lids are curled inwards in such a way that they are irritating the eyeball itself. The condition appears to be hereditary, and can only be put right by surgery. It is important to have this operation done, to save the animal a great deal of discomfort.

### External parasites

A dog that is allowed any sort of free-range exercise, even if only in the garden, is liable to pick up fleas, lice and ticks. There are many powders and sprays on the market that can get rid of these very quickly. To be successful, you should treat the bedding and any places where the dog habitually rests as well as the animal itself. Fleas and lice can lead to skin problems and general disability, so you should act immediately. Follow the instructions on the container, and the problem will soon be solved.

### Eyes

The eye is a very delicate organ, and when giving any treatment, you must take great care and never put any pressure on it. A slight discharge might be caused by the dog lying in a draught. Wipe the eye with cotton wool or a tissue soaked in a lukewarm boracic solution. If the condition does not clear up in a couple of days, then it might be something more serious which will need the attention of a veterinary surgeon.

If a foreign body, such as a grass seed, gets into the eye bathe it gently with a weak solution of Optrex and try to remove the particle.

If the dog somehow manages to get acid in its eyes, you should immediately use your fingers to make a purse of the eyelids and pour in some castor oil or glycerine. Then immediately take the dog to a veterinary surgeon.

### Feet

Split pads or eczema can make a dog nibble at its feet until it is lame. If this happens, apply gentian violet liberally, and allow time for the sores to heal.

Cysts between the toes can be a nuisance and always need veterinary treatment.

Torn dew claws and torn nails can be very uncomfortable for the dog. The paw can become very tender and make the dog quite lame. Soak the paw in an antiseptic solution as often as possible, as this will ease the pain. Try to keep the paw clean.

If your dog gets tar on its foot in hot weather, this should be removed as it can be very uncomfortable. Cut the hair away from between the toes and rub plenty of fat, such as lard or margarine into the toes to soften the tar. Then wash the foot.

### Fits

Fits are often associated with virus diseases. If they occur, you should consult your veterinary surgeon as soon as possible.

### Haematoma

This is a blood blister which is usually caused by a dog scratching itself. It can also be the result of a blow. Unlike an abcess, this swelling is soft at first, though a hard edge forms later. The condition is most likely to be found on a dog's ear, and if it does not clear up, surgery may be needed.

### Hard pad disease

Canine encephalitis, or 'hard pad', disease is caused by a virus. In many ways it is similar to distemper and, like distemper, it attacks the nervous system. Those animals that survive have a thickening or hardening of the skin on the pads of the feet, and sometimes on the nose. This is, of course, how the disease gets its name.

### Hiccoughs

Hiccoughs are most common in puppies, and are usually the result of indigestion or, sometimes, irritation caused by worms. It is not a serious complaint, but can be distressing to the dog while it lasts. Bicarbonate of soda in milk usually brings some relief.

### Hip displasia

Hip displasia is a malformation of the hip joint. It seems to affect some breeds more than others. It is a deformity which is difficult to diagnose without an X-ray. A dog may have a bad gait and be labelled as having hip displasia when in fact it is free of it, while another animal that seems to move quite well may actually be found to have it.

Dogs with hip displasia can live to a great age and be just as active as those with correct hips. The condition is not serious in a family pet, though the dog should not be bred from.

### Kennel cough

Kennel cough is found in boarding kennels and anywhere else where there are large numbers of dogs. It passes quickly from one dog to another and can put a show dog out of circulation for quite a long time. However, it is not a serious problem for adult dogs, who seem to be able to get over it quite easily. In puppies, however, it is more damaging. Kennel cough weakens them and takes a great toll on their general health, setting them back in their progress. If they get the disease, they should be given antibiotics by a veterinary surgeon to prevent any secondary infection. There are a variety of views as to how kennel cough should be treated, and progress is being made all the time, so if you have any worries it is a good idea to seek professional advice.

### Leptospirosis

There are two different types of leptosirosis.

One from is *leptospiral jaundice*. This is usually caused by food which has been fouled by virus-carrying rats. The symptoms are fever, diarrhoea, listlessness, bleeding gums and sometimes a bleeding nose. The actual jaundice does not become apparent until later. Urgent veterinary help is essential – but this is another example of a disease a puppy should be inoculated against early on.

The other form is *leptospiral nephritis*. This is a deadly disease that attacks the kidneys. Symptoms are a high temperature, lethargy and loss of appetite. The dog has a pain in its kidneys, which makes it roach its back and loin. It may have difficulty in passing urine, and it may have an excessive thirst and foul breath. Here again, inoculation beforehand is far better than a cure. There is little chance of recovery from either of these forms of leptospirosis.

### Metritis

Metritis is a condition that occurs in bitches after they have whelped. It is caused by the retention of membranes and afterbirth. Call a verterinary surgeon immediately, so that the bitch can have an injection of pituitrin, which will get rid of the waste. This will be followed by a course of antibiotics, to clear up any infection.

*Nettlerash (urticaria)*
Nettlerash is not serious, but can be worrying to an owner who has not seen it before. The dog's head swells, lumps appear all over its body, and it looks miserable. The condition, which is usually caused by some sort of allergy, tends to subside on its own quite quickly and does not require any treatment. It does not affect the dog's appetite or general well-being.

*Poisoning*
If you think that your dog has swallowed any poison, you should act quickly to get it out of the system. Simple emetics are best, such as washing soda or salt and water.

*Rabies*
Rabies is a very serious and dangerous disease which can affect all mammals. This of course includes humans as well as domestic and wild animals. In island countries, such as Britain, it has been possible to keep rabies out by maintaining strict laws on the import of animals. In other countries, this has not been possible.

Rabies is an acute, infectious disease, caused by a virus and transmitted by the saliva of an infected animal. When a rabid animals bites, the infected saliva contaminates the wound and enters the body of the new host. The first symptom of rabies in a dog may be a change of temperament. A difficult dog may become friendly, while an affectionate one may become excitable and bad tempered. In most cases, this stage is followed by the so-called 'dumb rabies', in which the dog becomes paralysed and unable to close its jaws. There will be a lot of saliva. Eventually, the dog dies of respiratory failure.

Suspected rabies should be notified immediately to the local veterinary officer and the police. A dog that has rabies must be destroyed at once.

It is possible to protect dogs against rabies by inoculation. Most rabies-free countries demand that imported mammals are made to spend a period of time in quarantine as soon as they enter the country.

*Rheumatism*
Like humans, dogs – especially older ones – can be subject to rheumatism and can suffer severe pain from a bad attack. Give the dog aspirins three or four times a day. This will alleviate the pain and help to cure the rheumatism.

*Rickets*
Rickets is more often found in larger breeds of dogs than in smaller ones. It usually means that a puppy's bones have not formed correctly, often as a result of malnutrition.

Knobbly, crooked joints, bowed legs and a generally malformed appearance are all signs of improper feeding and rearing. In the advanced stages, the bones become soft and are easily broken. Prevention, of course, is much better than a cure.

*Shock*
Shock can occur after a severe injury, or after any event that strongly affects the nervous system. The dog must be kept as quiet as possible, and warm. A dog that is not fully conscious should never be persuaded to swallow any liquid.

*Skin conditions*
Most skin troubles can be prevented, as they are very often the result of an owner's neglect or lack of observation. There are a great many preparations on the market today which can help keep a dog's coat in first-class condition, so there is really no justification for allowing a skin condition to develop.

Non-experts tend to label all skin conditions 'mange', whether or not a proper diagnosis has been made. This can only be done using a skin scraping. *Sarcoptic mange* is caused by a tiny parasite. It is contagious and easily spread through bedding, brushes, kennels and so on. It begins as small red spots, like flea bites, which attack the skin around the eyes, the outside of the ears and on the abdomen. These secrete acrid matter, setting up an intense irritation which makes the dog bite and scratch itself. This in turn creates sore and bare patches. The condition can easily be cured using modern drugs.

*Follicular mange* usually starts off with a single bare patch which is a dirty, greyish colour. Like sarcoptic mange, the condition is caused by parasites, but in this case there is no irritation. The parasite can be seen under a microscope, and looks like a small maggot. Some people believe that the condition is congenital and not contagious. It is much more difficult to cure than sarcoptic mange, and you should seek help from a veterinary surgeon.

*Snake bites*
If your dog is bitten by a dangerous snake, you must act at once. Apply a tourniquet between the bite and the heart. This will help stop the poison getting into the bloodstream. Open up the bite and push crystals of potassium permanganate into it and get the dog to a veterinary surgeon as fast as possible. Keep the dog as comfortable as possible, but speed is the essential factor. Try to identify the snake as well.

*Stings*
If a dog is stung by a bee, extract the sting as fast as possible, and then treat the area with TCP or bicarbonate of soda. A wasp sting, which will not have to be removed, should be treated with vinegar or acid, and in both cases it is advisable to have the animal injected with antihistamine.

*Sunstroke or heatstroke*
The signs of sunstroke are excessive panting and profuse salivation, followed by weakness of the limbs, a staggering gait and then complete collapse. Put the dog in a cool place and apply ice and cold water to its head, neck and shoulders. It is essential to act fast.

Sunstroke can be avoided if the dog always has a good supply of water and adequate shade, especially if it is kept in a run for long periods. Take special care if you have to leave your dog in a car. A dog should never be shut in on a hot day. (See *Some Precautions 2*, page 14.) If you do this, heatstroke or even death can easily result.

*Worms*
Almost all dogs have worms at some time in their lives. Puppies are likely to suffer from roundworms (*Toxocara canis*), and they should all be treated for these when they are young. Adult dogs suffer more from tapeworms, which tend to make them lose condition, especially in the coat, scratch continually and have foul-smelling breath. The appetite may either increase or decrease.

Worms tend to pull a dog's health down very quickly, so you should act at once if you see any symptoms. The two types have different treatments, so you should try to work out which kind they are so that you can use the right remedy. There a number of these on the market and, as long as you follow the instructions on the packet, they are quite safe. It is a good idea to treat a dog for worms from time to time anyway, whether or not you have seen any. This can do no harm as long as the treatment is administered in the right dose.

Although roundworms and tapeworms are the most common, there are other worms, such as whipworms, hookworms and heartworms. If your dog does not respond to treatment for worms, it is a good idea to send a specimen of its faeces to your veterinary surgeon for analysis. It may have some of the more unusual worms and you will need a stronger medicine to get rid of them.

# FEEDING

Any advice on feeding given in a book of this kind must be very general. The amount of food a dog needs at any stage of its life depends on a variety of factors: its size and breed are obvious ones, but there is also the question of how much exercise it gets and whether or not it tends to put on fat. Like humans, dogs vary from individual to individual when it comes to appetite! However, there are some basic rules.

## Your new puppy
When you bring your puppy home, it will probably be between eight and ten weeks old. At this stage, you should have a diet sheet from its breeder, and you should pay careful attention to this. All good breeders provide these sheets, and you should keep to the one you have as far as possible.

If you do not have such a sheet, the following general rules will prove useful.

A young puppy at the age of about eight weeks will need four meals a day, two of meat and biscuit and two milk-based. Milk based meals can be made from Farex and milk, semolina pudding, breakfast cereal with milk or proprietory baby cereal.

As the puppy matures it will gradually need fewer meals a day and will be less eager to eat so often. The first meal it will be less inclined to eat will probably be one of the milk ones.

As far as providing meat meals goes, there are several ways you can do this (see below) and each one can be as successful as the next. Provided you stick to the breeder's diet sheet, you can choose whichever method seems to suit you or your puppy best.

## Older puppies
As your puppy gets older, particularly if it is one of the bigger breeds, certain additions to the food can be helpful. Try giving your puppy egg once or twice a week. Large dogs may also benefit from having pure bone meal (not gardening bone meal) now and again.

With medium-sized dogs and toys, you can reduce the number of meals each day to three by the time your puppy is twelve weeks old. If you have a larger breed of dog, continue giving four meals a day for longer, as the puppy needs these to develop the necessary bone and substance.

By six months, medium and small breeds should be down to two meals a day, though larger puppies may still need three at this stage.

The point at which you cut down on the number of meals always depends ultimately on the individual puppy and, just as with a child, commonsense must always prevail!

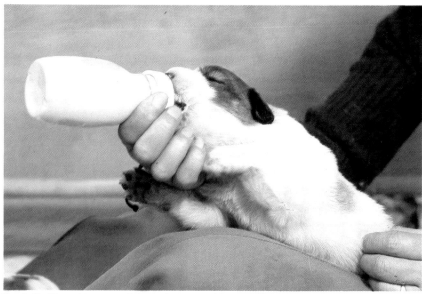
**Bottle feeding a Pyrenean Mountain puppy. Most will be weaned by seven weeks.**

## Problem eaters
If your puppy seems not to want the food you have offered it, take the dish away after a few minutes. This is especially important in the summer when there are flies around and likely to settle on it. Do not give the puppy a chance to become a faddy eater unless it is sick and has to be persuaded to eat. Even then, it is better not to leave the food sitting around, but instead hand-feed it. This means pushing the food down the puppy's throat – something that needs great care and patience.

Puppies are usually enthusiastic eaters and it takes a lot to put one off its food. But you should not forget just how bewildering a change of homes can be for a young puppy. Suddenly, it is alone, without its brothers and sisters, and all the familiar kennel smells of disinfectant and sawdust have gone. The only human hands the puppy has known so far have been the breeder's, but now there are all sorts of other people around, and a whole new selection of smells and sounds. All things considered, it is amazing that puppies do not take longer to get used to their new surroundings, and not at all surprising if, in the early days, they are not relaxed enough to eat heartily.

## Meat meals
One way to provide meat is to buy it ready-cooked. There are a number of good prepared cooked meats on the market, usually available from pet stores. Mix this meat with meal or biscuit, which is also available from pet stores and supermarkets.

Alternatively, if you have a good family butcher, you may be able to arrange for a supply of meat. Chicken

or rabbit is ideal. Cook the meat in water and then throw the bones away – a young puppy must never be allowed to have these. Soak the biscuit in the stock from the meat and then add the meat itself to the mixture.

Probably the most popular feeding method busy people use is to buy tinned food. These provide a carefully balanced, scientifically prepared diet. Tinned meat should also be served with soaked biscuit or puppy meal.

Lastly, there is dried dog food – another useful product to try.

## Adult dogs
The different ways of giving food to puppies apply also to adult dogs, for whom tins, prepared cooked meat, butcher's scraps and dried food are all possible options. The occasional marrow-bone is not only a useful way of keeping the teeth clean and healthy, but also gives a great deal of pleasure, and can do no harm. Do not give the dog raw bones, as these can chip and get stuck in its throat. As far as butcher's scraps go, tripe and trimmings from steak or lamb are suitable, and it is not necessary to cook these.

Never feed your dog on scraps of human food left over after your own meals. This can quickly lead to bad habits, and might harm the dog.

## Feeding dishes
Like the dish in which water should always be available for your dog, the food dish should be heavy and solid. It should not slip around while the dog is eating, and it should not be knocked over easily. After each meal, the dish should be washed. It should be kept for the dog alone to use.

# SHOWING YOUR DOG

When you bought your puppy, your probably had no intention of taking it to shows. But perhaps it has grown to look so good that someone suggests that it might be fun to take it to a local show. If you decide to do so, your first task is to find out about shows.

**Dog shows**
Dog shows are common events throughout Europe, North America and Australia, and are almost always held under the auspices of the kennel club in the country concerned. Among all the shows available to you, there is likely to be something for you and your puppy.

The best way to find out where the shows are is to consult one of the specialist magazines or contact your national kennel club. They will be able to tell you the name of your local secretary, who in turn can give you all the information you need.

The smaller shows are the best place for a beginner handler and a puppy to begin their show careers, and these provide a very good training ground.

Open shows are the next step up, followed by the Championship Shows, where the very best dogs will be found.

All Canine Societies run social events as well as their allocation of shows, and for a small fee you can become a member and have all the details of these sent to you. Joining a society is a good way of getting to know other people with the same interest in dogs as yourself, and will give you a chance to learn from them.

**How a show is run**
Before you actually take part in a dog show, it is a good idea to go to one as a visitor, so that you can find out how they are run. Write to the show secretary for a schedule, which will give you all the information you need. Remember that in all countries, if you are going to enter a dog at a show, it must be registered with the kennel club concerned. If this is not the case, the dog and any wins it might have accrued will be disqualified.

A show schedule gives details of all

the classes available. If you are starting at one of the smaller shows, you will probably find there are no Breed classes, and that you only have a choice of Variety classes.

At these smaller shows you will probably find that there is just one judging ring, which will be surrounded by chairs or rope. At the larger events, which can cover up to four days, there may be as many as forty rings. In Britain, these shows are always *benched*. This means that there is a bench available for each dog, where the animal is either put in a cage or secured with a benching chain. Kennel Club rules say that no dog should be off the bench except when it is being judged or exercised.

Whatever the size of the show, the same rules and regulations apply all over the world, and the details and information given in the schedule are strictly adhered to.

At the beginning of the show, the judge will enter the ring at the given time. There will usually be one or two

**Judging a variety of breeds at a small dog show.**

**A judge examines a selection of English Setters in a show ring.**

stewards to muster the dogs into the ring at the right time for the right class. All the classes are numbered in the schedule, and will be judged in that order. The stewards will have catalogues, so that they can check which dogs are present and enter the absentees in the judging book. The judge, however, will not have a catalogue until the judging is over. When the judging starts, the stewards retire to a corner of the ring.

Judging procedure usually follows a set pattern. Most judges like to have a look at the dogs in the class, and then they will ask them all to move around the ring. Each dog is then handled by the judge, who assesses the eyes, ears, mouth, teeth, overall balance of head and neck, the placement of the shoulders, the proportion of the back and loin, the quarters, the tail set and so on. Then the handler will be asked to move the dog, so that the judge can see it do this in profile.

When the judge has completed a class, he or she will place the dogs, from left to right, down to fourth or even fifth place, marking the judging book accordingly. After that, the lucky winners will be presented with their cards. Then the dogs, with their handlers, will leave the ring, and the stewards will call for the next class.

### What are the judges looking for?
There is a standard for every breed. Each judge of that breed is expected to

know that standard and apply it to various dogs. This is particularly important when a judge is awarding certificates at the Championship Shows. Each country has its own system for making up Champions, all varying in their particular methods. In Britain, for example, three certificates, one of which must be gained after the dog is twelve months old, entitle the dog to be known as a Champion – which is every breeder's ambition.

By judging to the standard, a judge should be able to recognize the type of animal he or she is looking for: the shape of the head, the body, legs and so on that belong to that one breed. As well as type, the judge must be able to see the correct conformation – how the animal is constructed and how it moves. The standard for each breed is quite definite on the way the dog should move. For example, one does not expect a Basset to move like a Terrier.

### Getting ready for a show
Preparing for a show is very important, and pays dividends on the day. Teach your puppy what will be expected of it at the show. This means that if it is the kind of dog that must be examined on a table, it must be prepared for this at home. Pose it on a table just as a judge would do, opening the mouth to look at the teeth, feeling the shoulders and legs, and going gently over the body down to the hindquarters. If it is the sort of dog that will be examined on the floor,

adopt a similar procedure. A little time spent this way each day will help it give its best when it is handled by a judge.

Walk the dog up and down on the show lead until it is proficient. If you can get it to stand on a loose lead without much handling, this is very helpful. A judge always likes to see a good dog able to show off its virtues without any assistance from the handler. Practice for a show will always help.

### Arriving at the show
One of the first things you should do when you arrive at a show is buy a catalogue. This will give you all the information you need, and you will be able to weigh up the opposition. Then make sure you find a comfortable and convenient spot for you and your dog. Most dogs nowadays travel in boxes or crates and it is easy to transfer one of these from your car to the show venue. The animal will feel safe and at home in its own house.

If it is a benched show, you should put the puppy on the bench marked for it. You will need a benching rug for it to rest on and a good safe benching chain to fix to the bench and on to the collar. The collar should be leather – never a choke chain.

You will also need the dog's show lead, which you will have been using for practice, and any grooming materials you will need to tidy it up at the last minute. Take a bowl for water, and food if the dog is a bad traveller.

Always make sure that you arrive at the show in good time, so that you and the dog can be well settled before you have to enter the ring.

At the larger shows and Championship events, you will be sent entrance passes by the show management, and these will tell you your bench number.

### After the judging
Do not be disappointed if you do not succeed at first, even when you know you have a good puppy. Speak to your fellow-exhibitors, especially those with the same breed of dog as yours. They will probably be able to help and advise you. When the judging is finished, it is perfectly permissible to ask the judge for his or her advice. Most will be only too happy to help a novice and to offer guidance to the virtues or otherwise of your dog.

The world of show dogs is large, but there is always room for newcomers. Of course, everyone wants to win – but with patience, and hard work, starting at the bottom, there is no doubt that a good dog will get the praise it deserves.

# BREEDING FROM YOUR DOG

If you have a pedigree bitch and decide to breed from her, it will almost certainly be an exciting and worthwhile exercise. Even professional breeders find this. They go to great lengths to plan litters, and almost as soon as a litter is born they may start to think about mates for them.

There is nothing certain about breeding dogs – or any animals for that matter – and even the most carefully planned litter can go wrong for no apparent reason at all. This is probably what makes breeding so fascinating.

### Finding the right mate

It will, naturally, be very important to you to find the right mate for your bitch. You should look for one who can tie in with her bloodlines. Do not simply choose the most convenient dog – the one nearest you or easiest to reach. Try to select a sire who will improve on your bitch and whose bloodlines will complement hers. If necessary, consult your bitch's breeder, who may be able to suggest a suitable dog.

*Line breeding*

One of the best ways to produce a quality animals is to use a method called *line breeding*. This is the breeding of two animals that are closely related, but not as closely as in inbreeding. Good results can be obtained, for example, by mating a half-brother with a half-sister, or a grandfather with a grand-daughter, or vice versa. This is the best way to establish 'type' according to the standard of the breed, and to improve the stock. Of course, you may be lucky if you mate from two completely unrelated animals, and produce very good dogs indeed, but these will rarely reproduce anything worthwhile themselves.

*Overall qualities*

As well as studying your bitch's pedigree, you should look for a dog of the same type as yours, with the same overall good qualities. He does not necessarily need to be a champion. Often, an outstanding stud dog may never have done well in the ring, usually because it (perhaps quite sensibly) does not like being shown.

Weigh up the virtues (and otherwise) of both the dog and the bitch very carefully. It is not only the appearance of the animals that matters, but what lies behind the pedigrees. It is a great help to know exactly what each pedigree looks like, and what were their virtues and faults. Established breeders, who can remember the backgrounds of pedigrees are usually only too happy to help a novice who is genuinely interested.

Any breeding stock should be quite free from outstanding faults and should be of the highest quality. Choose your stud dog carefully, with the aim of trying to improve your breed, rather that just to perpetuate it.

### When to mate the bitch

Different breeds of bitches come into season at different ages. Some of the toy breeds will have their first season as young as six or seven months, though they are nothing like mature at this age and should not be bred until at least their second season. The larger breeds, such as Irish Wolfhounds and Great Danes, may not come into season until they are about a year old, and should not be bred from until they are at least two, if not older. The breeder from whom you bought the bitch should be able to give you some advice, but the basic rule is that you should be sure your bitch is fully mature and both physically and mentally ready for motherhood before you have her mated.

If you are lucky and your bitch is winning well at shows, you may decide to make the best of this time and not have her mated until she is three or four. Delaying mating in this way does no harm at all. Most bitches get back into shape very well after having a litter, but some do not, and many people think it is a good idea to campaign a good show bitch to her championship before letting her have a litter.

On the other hand, some bitches are very slow to mature and will deepen in the body once they have had a litter and look much better for having had a family. In the end, only the owner can decide on the right time to have the bitch mated.

### Mating

A bitch is usually ready for mating between the eleventh and fourteenth day of her season, but this can vary enormously from bitch to bitch and from breed to breed. Some bitches have stood to be mated as early as their second or third day, and have had puppies, while others have been mated as late as the twentieth day and have had successful litters.

Watch the bitch very carefully while she is in season. She is likely to be ready to stand to the dog when her colour discharge begins to fade. When she is taken to the dog, she should willingly stand with her tail to one side, welcoming the dog. This is a good sign that she is ready.

Sometimes a bitch is very difficult and may try to bite the dog, and anyone who is trying to hold her. Since no one wants this to happen, it is a good idea to tape the mouth of a difficult bitch until a mating has been effected. After that, she is usually quite happy about the whole thing and the tape can be taken off. A bitch may make the whole process very difficult for the stud dog, but if he is experienced he will be able to overcome this. However, a young stud dog being used for the first time should never be put to a difficult bitch, or he may be put off altogether.

### Care during pregnancy

*Food*

The gestation period is sixty-three days after the mating, though puppies may be born as much as five or six days early or three or four days late. While the bitch is carrying her puppies she should have extra food. This should be given as extra meals, rather than a larger meal once a day. Start by giving her two meals a day and then, towards the end of her pregnancy, give her three meals. If she is carrying a big litter, she will not have room to eat a very large meal all in one go, and it could make her very uncomfortable. Her meat ration should be increased and her biscuit meal cut down. An egg or two each week will be good for her, and there should always be plenty of fresh, cold water.

*Exercise*

For the first four or five weeks of being in whelp, the bitch should be allowed to take her normal exercise. It is about this time that you will be able to detect the first signs of pregnancy. With some bitches, you cannot be certain until the last week, but most will show ample proof by the fifth week.

From the sixth or seventh week, the bitch should have less exercise and, at this stage, should not really be allowed to run up and down stairs. It is probably best to let the bitch suit herself as to how much exercise she gets, and she is unlikely to do anything too strenuous. However, it is important that she should be kept in good physical condition, and she should not be allowed to lie around all day and take no exercise at all.

### The birth

*Preparations*

Introduce the bitch to her whelping box about ten days before the litter is due. This box must be large enough for her to turn around in and there should be a rail around it, about five centimetres (two inches) from the floor. This will protect the whelps when the bitch lies down and can save any of them from being crushed. This can easily happen with a big litter, especially if the bitch is disturbed and confused.

Most breeders find that newspaper is the best material for whelping a bitch on. As she draws near to her whelping date, the bitch will get into the box and begin to tear the paper into shreds. She may do this for several days before she settles down to whelp. The box must be kept scrupulously clean at all times, with a temperature in the whelping quarters of about 21°C (70°F).

One of the best ways to keep the box warm is to use a strip heater under it, as this keeps the bed dry as well as warm. You could also use an overhead infra-red lamp during whelping and for a few days afterwards, as this gives the puppies a good start. However, it is not a good idea to keep this there for long as it can dry out their coats and creates a certain amount of scurf. It is probably better, once the puppies have been born, to shut down the lid of the box heater and retain the under-box heater. Make sure that whenever you use an electrical appliance, neither the bitch nor her puppies can get hold of the wires.

*Labour*
The first true signs of labour are when you actually see the bitch push and strain. Take her temperature at this stage – it should be about two degrees below normal.

The bitch will continue to strain at regular intervals, and when this becomes more frequent and increases in intensity, a water bag should appear. Try not to disturb the bitch during this period, though you should keep an unobtrusive eye on her. Bitches are usually very capable of attending to their own whelpings, and some get quite upset if they are disturbed, even by their owners. If you suspect there are problems, though, do not hesitate to get in touch with your veterinary surgeon (who you should have warned beforehand that your bitch is due to whelp). Unless you are very experienced, you should never try to interfere yourself.

If everything seems to be going well, give the bitch a little hot milk between whelps. If it is a big litter, the paper will become saturated and nasty, and she will be more comfortable if you take the old paper away carefully, and put some clean paper under her.

Try to have someone with you that your bitch knows well, as it is always a good idea to have some help.

*After the birth*
As each puppy is born, there is an afterbirth attached to it. Most bitches will eat this as they break off the umbilical cord. This is quite normal.

When you think the bitch has finished whelping, she should be persuaded to leave her young and go for a walk in the garden. She will be reluctant to do this, but she will feel much more comfortable after she has relieved herself.

While this is being done, the person helping you can very quickly clean the bed. Replace the newspaper with specially prepared, hygienic shredded paper (available from pet shops) which the bitch can use to make a comfortable nest for herself and her young. At the same time as this is being done the puppies can be counted and each one's sex determined.

Before the bitch returns to her family, wash her down behind with warm water and dry her off thoroughly. This should make her feel happy and settled. She will return to her young and quickly start feeding them.

Handle the whelps as little as possible at this stage, or you may upset the dam and make her restless. She may even start to cover them up with paper or pick them up in her mouth and walk around the whelping box with them. If she does this, she is obviously disturbed, and the best thing you can do is leave her alone, possibly watching from an outside window.

For the first few days, the bitch will be unhappy about leaving her nest, but she must be taken out, so that she can relieve herself. Some slight discharge may occur after whelping, but this is quite normal, unless it goes on for more than a week, in which case veterinary advice should be sought.

Most bitches make very good mothers and make an excellent job of rearing their young. But they have their own needs, and will love the extra care you give them at this time – to say nothing of the extra food.

**Problems**
Some bitches suffer from *uterine inertia*. This means a complete absence of labour pains, which means the bitch will need help in giving birth. Pituitrin (administered by a veterinary surgeon) can help induce labour, but if this does not work, she will have to have an Caesarean operation. If the bitch is attended to in good time, before she is exhausted, the operation should be quite successful and she should be able to rear her puppies perfectly well. The fact that she has had the operation does not mean she will not be able to have another litter. In fact, the litter could be delivered perfectly normally.

If at any time an unpleasant smell comes from the vagina, send for your veterinary surgeon straight away, as this could mean there is still afterbirth in the bitch's body, or even a dead puppy. This can easily be sorted out with an injection of pituitrin.

If your bitch does not settle down to the job of looking after her puppies, and appears restless, you can be sure that something is wrong, and you should contact your veterinary surgeon at once.

**The puppies**

*Dew claws and tails*
At about three days, the whelps should have their dew claws removed and, if required, their tails docked. These jobs must be done by a professional and under no circumstances should be attempted by the novice breeder. An amateur may think that he or she has cut out most of a dew claw, only to find that this was not the case and it grows back again. With tails, it is of course essential that the correct length is cut, according to the demands of standard.

While these tasks are being done, the bitch should be removed from her box and taken out for a walk, so that she will not be disturbed by her puppies' cries.

*Nails*
Puppies' nails should be cut at least once a week. They grow very quickly when they are feeding from the bitch and not walking about at all. If they are not carefully trimmed, their mother's stomach becomes a mass of scratches they inflict as they try to get to her teats. Once the puppies are up on their legs and walking about on a hard surface, this job is not so necessary.

*Worming*
Puppies should be wormed at three weeks old, and again at five weeks. If they are harbouring worms, this will stunt their growth. Worming medicine can be bought from either your veterinary surgeon or a pet shop.

*Weaning*
Puppies in most breeds are ready to be weaned when they are about three weeks old, though if it is a big litter, this should start earlier. Weaning is a gradual process, and should not be hurried, or the puppies will have digestive problems.

At three weeks, offer them a little scraped raw meat once a day. They will quickly accept and enjoy this. After about three days, introduce two of these snacks of raw, scraped meat, adding to it each time.

From this, they can graduate to a

A litter of Golden Retrievers. This is an exhausting time for the mother who should be given plenty of attention as well as extra food.

milk food meal, so that they are now having two meat meals a day and one milk meal. Eating the milk meal can be rather messy at first, as they will keep falling into it, but they will get the hang of it in the end. Keep an eye out for the greedy ones, and make sure every puppy gets its share.

Gradually, take the strain from the dam so that, by six weeks, the puppies are having two milk meals a day and two meat meals. At seven weeks they should be weaned altogether and the dam taken away from them. She may wish to go back to them at night for two or three nights but really, she should be kept away from them altogether.

At this point you will have to help build her up again, and also to make sure that her milk glands have gone back to normal and that there is no sign of mastitis. Worm, bathe and groom her to make her feel really good again.

At eight weeks, the puppies will be old enough to go to their new homes, which will certainly be a sad time for everyone.

**Children at the birth**
If you have children of your own and your bitch as been their companion, it is exciting and informative for them to watch the whelps arriving. This should, of course, be done discreetly, without disturbing the bitch.

As the whelps grow up, the children can be given little jobs to do for the dam, so that they feel they are playing a part in helping the new lives they have watched being born. They will soon become very attached to the puppies and will know them all individually. This can, of course, create problems when the time comes to say 'goodbye', and the puppies go to their new homes.

27

# GLOSSARY

**affixes** normally attached to a dog's name in order to identify it with a particular kennel, and may consist of words added before or after other names. The kennel owner pays an annual fee to the Kennel Club for this title.

**apple-headed** a rounded or very domed skull.

**bad doer** a dog that will not put on any condition, no matter how well it is cared for. It will probably also be a poor eater.

**balance** every part of the body in proportion throughout.

**B. of B.** (abbreviation) Best of Breed

**benched show** a show where all the dogs are shown secured to a bench.

**bitch** a female dog.

**bite** the position of the lower and upper teeth when the mouth is shut.

**blaze** a white line or marking that runs down the face from the skull to the **muzzle.**

**bloom** the shine on a coat that is beautifully glossy.

**brace** two dogs of the same breed.

**brisket** the part of the body in front of the **chest** and between the forelegs.

**brood bitch** a **bitch** that is well-bred and kept for breeding purposes.

**butterfly nose** a nose that is spotted or speckled with flesh colour. In puppies, this often clears with age, so that the nose eventually becomes all black by the time the dog is adult.

**canine tooth** the long tooth placed behind the **incisors** on each side of the **jaw.**

**canter** an easy gallop.

**castrate** to surgically remove a dog's testicles.

**cat foot** a compact, tightly closed foot that resembles that of a cat.

**C.C.** (abbreviation) Challenge Certificate.

**Champion** a dog that has qualified according to an individual country's rules and gained the required points for championship honours.

**character** the make-up of a dog – the combination of all essential points of appearance, disposition and behaviour.

**cheeky** rather thick, rounded, protruding cheeks.

**chest** the part of the body above the **brisket** and between the shoulder blades.

**chiselled** clean cut in the head, with the **muzzle** well modelled conforming to the breed standard.

**choke collar** a chain, leather or nylon collar that loosens or tightens as the **handler** requires.

**chops** the lower cheeks, **jaws,** lips and mouth.

**clipping** when the dog moves its front legs are struck by his back feet.

**cloddy** thick set, short and rather heavy.

**close-coupled** short from the last rib to the hip bone.

**cobby** a compact dog.

**condition** general health, coat and appearance.

**conformation** the general structural make-up of a dog.

**covering ground** the amount of ground covered between the forelegs and rear legs while the animal is on the move.

**cow-hocked** a serious fault, where the animal bends its **hocks** inwards.

**crabbing** when a dog moves sideways with its body at an angle to the line of progress. The rear legs thus go past the front feet, but without **clipping** them.

**cross-bred** the result of mating between two dogs of different breeds.

**croup** the back, immediately before the root of the tail.

**cryptorchid** a male animal that does not have its testicles properly descended into the scrotum.

**dam** the mother of a dog.

**dew claw** extra claw that is found on the inside of the lower portion of the legs. These are best removed a few days after birth.

**dish face** a concave **muzzle,** as in a Pointer.

**dock** to shorten the tail surgically.

**doggy** a term used to describe a **bitch** that is too masculine.

**down in pasterns** the front feet come forward at an angle instead of coming down in a straight line from the **forearm,** making them appear bent at the pasterns.

**dual champion** a dog in the U.K. that has not only qualified in the show ring, but also for a working certificate as a gun-dog in the field.

**elbow** the joint at the top of the **forearm.**

**elbows out** when the **elbows** turn out from the body.

**ewe neck** a fault in which the neck is thin and over-arched.

**expression** a combination of the features of the head, particularly the eyes.

**false heat** when a **bitch** appears to think she is **in season** and acts accordingly. Mating, though, is usually unsuccessful.

**flat-sided** a dog with a flat rib-cage – not rounded.

**flews** pendulous lips.

**forearm** the long bone of the front leg, between the **elbow** and the **pastern.**

**foreface,** the front of the face, or **muzzle.**

**forehand** the front of a dog, excluding the head.

**gait** the movement of the dog.

**gay stern** a tail that is carried higher than the standard demands, sometimes even curling over the back.

**hackney action** when the front legs are lifted high, in the manner of a hackney horse.

**handler** the person in charge of a dog.

**hare foot** a long, narrow, oval foot.

**haw** the inner part of the lower eyelid.

**heat** the term used to describe a bitch in **season.**

**height** the measurement of a dog from the withers to the ground.

**hocks** the joints in the hind legs between the pasterns and the stifles.

**hocks well let down** when the **hocks** are close to the ground.

**hound-marked** the characteristics of Beagles, Harriers and Foxhounds.

**in-breeding** the mating of two closely-related dogs, such as father and daughter.

**incisors** the front teeth between the **canine** teeth.

**jaws** the upper and lower part of the **foreface** where the teeth are placed.

**kennel blindness** the inability of a kennel owner to see any faults in his or her own dogs, or any virtue in other people's dogs.

**knuckling over** the front legs bulging over at the **pastern.**

**leather** the skin of the pendant ear flap.

**leggy** legs that are too long for the dog and out of **balance** with the rest of the body.

**level bite** when the upper and lower **incisors** meet edge to edge.

**line breeding** the mating of two dogs with similar strains, but not too closely related, such as a grandfather and grand-daughter or half brother and half sister.

**lippy** when lips overhang, or are more developed than they should be.

**litter** puppies born at one **whelping** of a **bitch.**

**loaded shoulders** a general heaviness of the **shoulders.**

**loin** the part of the body between the last rib and the hindquarters.

**mating** putting together a male and female for purposes of reproduction.

**milk teeth** the **puppy** teeth.

**molar teeth** the rear teeth, used for grinding food.

**mongrel** a dog of mixed ancestry, carrying the bloodlines of several purebred dogs of different breeds or of mixed parentage themselves.

**monorchid** a male animal with only one testicle in the scrotum.

**muzzle** the **foreface,** the nose and jaws.

**N.F.C.** (abbreviation) Not For Competition. This refers to dogs entered in a show for display purposes only, and not for competition.

**occiput** the upper back point of the skull.

**oestrum** the period of the **season** in which a **bitch** may be mated.

**out at elbows** when the **elbows** are turned out from the body.

**out at shoulders** when the shoulder blades are rather wide and appear loosely attached to the body.

**overshot** when the front teeth project over and beyond the bottom teeth.

**paddling** when the dog throws its front feet out sideways in a rather loose and uncontrolled manner.

**pads** the cushioned soles of the dog's foot.

**pastern** the lowest part of the front leg.

**patella** a cap-like bone, similar to the knee in a person, at the **stifle** joint.

**pedigree** table of genealogy giving the ancestry of the dog.

**pelvis** a cage-like set of bones attached to the end of the spinal column providing the foundation for the back legs.

**period of gestation** time taken by a **bitch** to produce her **litter** – usually about 63 days.

**pied** a term used for a coat with two or three colours in the mixture.

**pigeon-toed** when the forefeet incline towards each other.

**pile** thick undercoat of soft hair.

**prefix** attached to the front of a dog's name, indicating the kennel from which it has come.

**premolar teeth** the small teeth that are placed between the large back teeth and the **canine** teeth.

**puppy** a dog less than a year old.

**quarters** the hind legs.

**racy** rather slight in build, with long legs and body.

**rangy** long in tail and body and rather loose-limbed, but with greater bone and body than a dog that is **racy.**

**rat tail** a thin tail that has short, smooth hair.

**reachy** covering a lot of ground between the front and hind feet.

**ribbed up** a compact dog with well-rounded and well-formed ribs.

**rickets** a disease of the bone usually caused by bad rearing.

**ring** the area in which the judge assesses the dogs at a show.

**roach back** an arched back.

**Roman nose** a nose in which the tip turns down and back.

**saddle** coloured marking over the back, like a saddle.

**saddle-backed** a back that dips in the middle.

**scissor bite** when the **incisors** of the upper **jaw** just overlap those on the lower.

**season** the term used to describe a bitch's period of **oestrum** when she may be successfully **mated.**

**second thigh** the muscular development of the legs between the **stifles** and the **hocks.**

**septum** the very thin division between the nostrils.

**service** the term given to the mating of a bitch by the dog.

**set-on** where the root of the tail meets the body.

**shelly** lacking bone, body and power throughout.

**short-coupled** short and compact between the last rib and hip joint.

**shoulder** the area around the shoulder blade and the muscles that support it.

**sickle hocks** when **hocks** are so bent that the part below them is placed forward, not vertical.

**sire** the male parent of a **litter.**

**slab-sided** flat sides, with flat ribs.

**sloping shoulders** shoulders that are well laid back, allowing the dog to move properly and efficiently.

**snipy** a weak, narrow **muzzle.**

**spay** a surgical operation to prevent a bitch from conceiving.

**splay foot** a flat foot with spreading toes.

**standard** the official description of the breed to which dogs should be judged.

**stern** the tail of any hound.

**stifle** the joint in the hind leg, between the thigh and the **second thigh.**

**stop** the depression between the eyes and dividing the forehead and the **muzzle.**

**undercoat** soft, short hair, concealed by a longer coat.

**undershot** having the lower **incisors** projecting beyond the upper **incisors.**

**upper arm** the part between the **elbow** and **shoulder.**

**weaving** when the front legs cross as the dog moves.

**weediness** lightly formed throughout.

**whelp** a very young **puppy.**

**whelping** the act of giving birth to **puppies.**

**withers** the highest part of the body, just behind the neck and from where the top of the shoulder blades may be felt.

**wrinkle** loose skin on the skull and sides of the face.

# AFGHAN HOUND

*Hound group*

**Size**
Males: 68–74 cm (27–29 ins)
Females: 63–69 cm (25–27 ins)

**Coat**
Long, with very fine texture on the ribs, fore- and hindquarters and flanks. In mature dogs, the hair should be short and close along the saddle. In the foreface, the hair is short. It is long from the forehead back, with a distinct, silky top-knot. The pasterns can be bare. It is important that the coat is allowed to develop naturally.

**Colour**
All colours are acceptable.

**Grooming**
Grooming is of the utmost importance, and there is no short-cut to doing this job properly. Use a nylon and bristle brush, followed by combing out with a good metal dog comb. Do this thoroughly, once a week.

**Exercise**
As a growing puppy, the Afghan should never be over-exercised. Until it is about four months old, it can get all the exercise it needs in its own home and garden. As it gets older, it will need more proper exercise, which should include good free exercise in an open space as well as controlled exercise on a lead.

**Temperament**
Afghans should be aloof and dignified, but also gay and happy. They should not be shy.

**Suitability as a family companion**
Afghans are very suitable as family dogs: they are good guard dogs and good with children.

**Special needs**
Afghans need plenty of space if they are to be comfortably housed. You must have enough time to give your dog the exercise it needs.

As its name implies, this dog originated in Afghanistan. It is now popular all over the world. It its native land it is a working dog, used for guarding tents and homes and for hunting the gazelle by night. In India, it is used to guard flocks of sheep.

The whole appearance of the dog should be of strength and dignity. The head is long, but not too narrow, surmounted by a long top-knot of hair. The nose should preferably be black and the eyes should appear somewhat triangular. They should be dark.

Because it originated in desert areas, the Afghan's feet had to be large and strong in order to move well in the sand. This should still be looked for in the breed today. The tail is set low, has a ring at the end and is sparsely feathered. It should not be too short.

# AIREDALE

*Terrier group*

### Size
Males: 58–61 cm (23–24 ins)
Females: 56–58 cm (22–23 ins)

### Coat
The topcoat is hard, wiry and stiff, but not so long as to appear ragged. It should be straight and close, covering the body and legs. The undercoat is a shorter growth of softer hair. Some of the hardest coats are crinkly or just slightly waved, but a curly coat is completely wrong.

### Colour
Black-and-tan, which should be tan on the head and ears with the exception of dark markings on each side of the skull. The ears are a darker shade of tan than the rest. The legs are also tan up to the thighs and elbows. The body has a black or grizzle saddle effect.

### Grooming
Like all breeds that need regular trimming or grooming, the Airedale should become used to this procedure from early puppyhood. It is easiest to stand the dog on a table for a grooming session: the brush and comb should go right down to the skin. The coat will need stripping at least twice a year. This is best done by a professional.

### Exercise
The Airedale is a big, strong breed and, as an adult, it will need plenty of exercise, both controlled and free. Until it is about six months old, it will get all it needs within the home and garden. After that, more serious and regular daily exercise may begin. As with all puppies, when it has tired itself out it must be left to rest undisturbed.

### Temperament
The Airedale has been dubbed the 'King of Terriers', and it is certainly a very proud dog as shown in its eyes and the carriage of its ears and tail.

### Suitability as a family companion
This is a splendid, sturdy and adaptable family dog, good with children and excellent as a guard. It fits in well, both in a town flat or in the country.

### Special needs
The coat needs regular attention, as described above, and one must also appreciate that exercise is essential to keep the dog in good shape and fit.

The Airedale is the largest dog in the terrier group. It originated about a century ago in Yorkshire, where it was developed to tackle rats and otters in the Wharfe and Aire rivers. Its rough coat and willingness to cope with water were essential for its work. It was probably descended from the Otterhound and the old Black and Tan Terrier.

The eyes should be dark, small and full of terrier expression: keen and intelligent. The neat ears are carried at the side of the head. There is only a little difference between the length of the skull and the foreface. It should not have bulging cheeks.

The body is short, the thighs long, powerful and muscular. The feet are round, compact and neat. The tail is customarily docked and should be set on high and carried gaily – though it should never curl over the back.

The Airedale is attractive and sturdy as a puppy, and is equally so as an adult. It had a wonderful character: reliable, intelligent and sensible as a guard. It is loyal to its owner and household.

# AUSTRALIAN TERRIER

*Terrier group*

**Size**
Males and females: 25 cm (10 ins)
approx, 6.3 kg (14 lbs)

**Coat**
Harsh, straight, dense and
weatherproof. The body coat is about
6cm (2.5 ins) long with a good soft
textured undercoat. The hair on the
muzzle, ears, lower legs and feet is
somewhat shorter. There should be a
definite ruff around the neck.

**Colour**
There are two distinct colours: blue-
and-tan, or all red. With the blue-and-
tan, the main body colour is steel blue
or a dark grey-blue with rich tan on the
face, ears, underbody, lower part of the
legs and feet and under the tail. The
richer and more clearly defined the
colours are, the better. The soft silky
top-knot is blue, silver or a lighter shade

than the main head colour. The reds
should be a clear colour throughout, in
no way shaded or smutty.

**Grooming**
Although this sturdy, rugged, low-to-
ground terrier has an untrimmed coat,
regular brushing and combing will
enhance the appearance. It should
certainly not look shaggy or unkempt.

**Exercise**
The well built body and sturdy legs will
cope with sensible exercise, either in the
garden or a run in the park.

**Temperament**
Sensible, with the sharpness and
alertness associated with terriers.

**Suitability as a family companion**
The Australian Terrier is sociable, loyal
and even in disposition. It is a good
watchdog, and very suitable as a family
companion.

The Australian Terrier originated with
the early settlers in Tasmania. Its
ancestors were thought to be a small
rough coated blue-and-tan terrier, with
the Dandie Dinmont, Skye and Scottish
Terriers also playing a part. The
Yorkshire Terrier has probably also
been used in the breed's development. It
is essentially a working terrier. It is low-
set, rather long in proportion to its
height. It is strong in character, alert,
active and sensible. As the dog was used
to catch vermin, its muzzle should be
strong and powerful, and the same
length as the skull. The dark brown eyes
are small and keen, the ears are small,
neat and upright. The front legs are
straight and the hindquarters strong and
muscular. The tail is customarily
docked, set-on high and well carried.

The Australian has a free, springy,
forceful movement. The puppies are
sturdy and sound, and they grow up to
be so as adults.

# BASENJI

*Hound group*

### Size
Males: 43cm (17 ins) 10.6kg (24 lbs)
Females: 40cm (16 ins) 9.5kg (21 lbs)

### Coat
Short and sleek, with a silky texture.

### Colour
Bright red, black or black-and-tan, all with white feet, chest and tail tip. White legs, collar and blaze are optional.

### Grooming
The Basenji needs straightforward regular brushing with a hound glove. Finish it off with a soft cloth.

### Exercise
This is a hunting dog, which needs plenty of exercise. Bear in mind that puppies should never be over-exercised, but allowed to develop naturally within their own home and garden.

### Temperament
This breed is suspicious of strangers, but should not be shy.

### Suitability as a family companion
With its clean lines and non-doggy smell, the Basenji is gaining favour as a family dog.

The Basenji originated as a hunting dog in southern Sudan and Zaire. It may even be the type of dog we see on Egyptian friezes, which are over 5,000 years old. This dog does not bark, but instead makes a chortling, yodelling sound.

This is a well balanced dog with a gazelle-like grace: lightly-built, finely-boned and high on the leg. The puzzled frown, caused by fine wrinkles on the forehead, is a prized feature of the breed's expression. The neat, slightly hooded, prick ears, arched neck, lithe shape, tightly-curled tail and an easy-flowing movement all combine to give the dog the appearance of being graceful, attractive and clean-limbed.

The Basenji puppy is full of fun, as well as being extremely clean and easy to housetrain. It is a family dog, which must have firm but kind treatment.

# BASSET GRIFFON VENDEEN

*Hound group*

**Size**
This breed comes in two sizes:
*Standard:* 37.5–40.5 cm (15–16 ins)
*Petite:* 33–38 cm (13–15 ins)

**Coat**
Rough and shaggy, with a harsh texture, never silky or woolly. It should not be excessively long or abundant.

**Colour**
More or less dark fawn, hare-coloured or grey-white, or grey and white, orange-and-white, tan-and-white, black-and-white, or tri-coloured.

**Grooming**
The Vendeen's grooming needs are straightforward: a comb and good rub over with a hound glove and tidying any over-long hair will be quite adequate.

**Exercise**
This is a hunting breed which enjoys a good free run and plenty of exercise.

**Temperament**
Friendly and attentive.

**Suitability as a family companion**
The Vendeen is growing in popularity and is proving adaptable to family life. Its pleasant nature makes it good with children, ideal for an active, sporting family.

**Special needs**
There are no real problems with this breed, though the ears need to be checked for excess wax. Do not let the nails grow too long.

This is one of the many hunting hounds of France. It was used either in a pack, or alone for small and large game. It is similar to the Basset, but with a less exaggerated expression.

The body is slightly elongated, with a fairly deep chest. The front legs are straight and well boned. The hindquarters are muscular and slightly rounded. The feet are large and tight, with a hard sole. The tail is set on high, fairly long, thick at the root and tapering evenly to the tip.

Smart, cheerful and alert, the Vendeen is a rough-coated sporting hound that fits in well in the country and suburbs.

# BASSET HOUND

*Hound group*

**Size**
Males and females: 33–38 cm (13–15 ins)

**Coat**
Short, dense and weather-resisting.

**Colour**
Mainly tricolour (black, white and tan) or lemon-and-white, but any recognized hound colour is acceptable.

**Grooming**
A Basset needs regular brushing with a hound glove. The skin should be loose and elastic.

**Exercise**
This is a short-legged hound of considerable substance. It should be able to have regular exercise to keep it in good fettle, but should never be over-exercised. As a puppy it should be able to obtain its exercise in the freedom of the garden, and as it grows and develops it will need walks, with the opportunity to run loose in open spaces.

**Temperament**
Devoted and mild, in no way either timid or belligerent.

**Suitability as a family companion**
Delightful as this dog is, it will really only suit a family that lives in the country. It should not be kept in a flat or in the centre of a town.

**Special needs**
The Basset has a big frame and the puppy has a lot of growing to do. Exercise and feeding should reflect this, but the former should not be overtaxing.

The Basset originated in France. It was selectively bred by sportsmen in Britain for over a hundred years, more recently with the addition of American blood.

The Basset Hound should be full of quality, with a lean head and no snipiness in the muzzle. There should be a moderate amount of wrinkle at the brows and beside the eyes: the skin should be loose enough to wrinkle when the head is bent forward. The eyes are brown, soft and sad, slightly sunken but not too deeply set. The ears are extremely long, low set and curling inwards. They should be able to reach to the end of the muzzle. The tail is carried high, in the hound fashion.

The Basset is well bodied with plenty of heart and lung room and heavy bone. It moves deliberately, smoothly and with freedom. It is capable of great endurance in the hunting field.

# BEAGLE

*Hound group*

**Size**
Males and females: not less than 32.5 cm (13 ins) or more than 40 cm (16 ins)

**Coat**
Dense, smooth, weatherproof and short.

**Colour**
Beagles can be almost any colour or colours and be correctly marked. Liver-and-white is the only objectionable colour. It is often thought that the tri-colour (a combination of black, white and tan) is the only correct colour, but this is not so. The tail should always be tipped white. This is so that, when hunting, the hound may always be seen, even in the poorest weather.

**Grooming**
Although a short-haired breed, the Beagle enjoys regular grooming sessions with a hound glove, especially when it is moulting. It will also benefit from a spirit shampoo. Pay attention to keeping the ears clean.

**Exercise**
The Beagle is an active breed and, as such, it requires regular and sensible exercise. It benefits from, and enjoys long walks and free-range exercise. Puppies should not get overtired.

**Temperament**
Intelligent, alert and active. Beagles have an even temperament and are not aggressive. At times, they can be determined and strong-willed.

**Suitability as a family companion**
The merry Beagle is a most attractive and conveniently-sized hound. It adapts well to a modern home and is good with children. It needs to be kept occupied, or it becomes bored – which can have disastrous results.

**Special needs**
The Beagle's most important need is adequate exercise.

The Beagle's origins are ancient. It is the smallest of English hounds, and is steadily growing in popularity.

Compact, sturdy and well built, it has splendid proportions and clean lines without any sign of coarseness. Its expression is mild and kind, the eyes should not be deep set or bulgy. The ears (or *leathers*) should be long and of fine texture, ideally they should reach to the tip of the nose when extended. The body should be compact and sturdy with a good depth of chest and strong hindquarters. The tail (or *stern*) should be thick and well covered with hair at the end (the *brush*), it should always be carried gaily. The movement is one that is free-striding, long-reaching with drive from the hind legs.

Given lots of attention, exercise, good food and company the Beagle makes a smart and splendid pet.

# BEARDED COLLIE

*Working group*

**Size**
Males: 53–56 cm (21–22 ins)
Females: 51–53 cm (20–21 ins)

**Coat**
Double-coated, with a harsh, strong, flat outercoat and soft, dense undercoat. This should be free from woolliness and curl, but a slight wave is permissible. It should be long enough to give protection against the weather and to enhance the shape, but it should not obscure the natural body lines. It should not be trimmed in any way. Although the face typically has a beard, the eyebrows should not obscure the eyes.

**Colour**
One group of colours ranges from pale silver through all shades of grey to black. These are all born black and have black pigment. Other colours are: blue (born blue, with blue pigment), brown (born brown with brown pigment), and fawn or sandy (born light fawn with fawn pigment). All are with or without white markings. Where white occurs, it should be as a blaze on the face, and not encroach upon the eyes or ears. The chest and neck carry white in varying degrees. The neck may be entirely white but this should not extend further back than the shoulder. The legs may carry white and the tail tip is usually white. All the recognized colours are also permitted to be combined with tri-colour: the additional tan colour occuring where the white joins the main body colour on the cheeks and legs and beneath the tail. This tan should be very pale, to the point of being almost invisible, and should appear in small quantities only.

**Grooming**
Like all coated breeds, the Bearded Collie needs regular grooming from puppyhood. Make sure you brush right down to the skin. It should not be trimmed.

**Exercise**
This is a lean, active dog with boundless energy. Regardless of the weather, it enjoys exercise in the garden and sensible walks with some free running. It needs a good walk each day.

**Temperament**
This is a happy, bouncy, self-confident and lively dog. It is intelligent and sensible and shows no signs of nervousness or aggressiveness.

**Suitability as a family companion**
This dog is very suitable for most families as it is good with young children, adaptable and responsive to human company.

**Special needs**
This dog needs a lot of exercise. Its coat will need regular attention and the occasional bath.

This is an ancient breed that once worked with sheep in the hills and lowlands of Scotland. The Bearded Collie was especially valued for its splendid herding and droving qualities and its resistance to the severe Scottish winter weather.

The Bearded Collie is longer than it is high. It should not look too heavy, but should be lean and gracefully built. It should have a bright, enquiring expression. The eye colour should tone in with the main body colour and the eyes should be set wide apart, large, soft and affectionate.

The head should be in proportion to the size of the dog, and the muzzle should be strong. The nose and pigment should be black, but will generally follow the body colour in blues and browns.

The back is level and the tail is low-set, well covered with hair and reaching to the point of the hock. It should never be carried over the back. The movement should be free and flowing, with little effort: the legs lifting minimally from the ground.

# BEDLINGTON TERRIER

*Terrier group*

## Size
Males and females: about 41 cm (16 ins)
8–10.4 kg (18–23 lbs)
Males are usually slightly taller, females slighty shorter.

## Coat
The coat is quite distinctive. It is double-thick and linty, with harder guard hairs, which give it a 'textured' feel. The coat stands out well from the skin and has a tendency to twist, especially on the head and face. Some coats have a tighter twist than others. It does not shed.

## Colour
Bedlingtons can be blue or liver. The blues are born black and start to change into the adult blue at three months. The livers are chocolate at birth and also start to change at three months. Eye and pigment colour should be as dark as possible and match the main body colour.

## Grooming
Unlike most terriers, the Bedlington is not stripped. Instead, it is clipped or scissored into shape, the hair usually being kept fairly short. Regular brushing and combing is essential.

## Exercise
This dog will exercise itself within a reasonably-sized garden. It enjoys walks and loves a gallop, but it must be supervised.

## Temperament
The Bedlington is quiet and gentle but, like all terriers, it can be roused. It should not be shy or nervous.

## Suitability as a family companion
This dog is an ideal size and is adaptable and good with children. It has a non-shedding coat and is contented in the house.

## Special needs
Grooming is important, as the new hair grows into the old and if it is neglected, it will matt and tangle.

The Bedlington originated in the north of England and takes its name from the mining village of Bedlington. The Dandie Dinmont and the Whippet are both part of its ancestry. It originated as a working terrier, capable of killing all kinds of vermin.

It is a graceful, lithe and muscular dog, capable of galloping at great speed. At walking pace, its rather mincing, light and springy movement is quite distinctive. It is important that a Bedlington has what experts refer to as a *horse-shoe front*: being wider at the chest than at the feet.

The head is pear-shaped, and the expression mild and gentle. When roused, the dog should look full of temper and courage.

The back is roached and the loins gently arched, with muscular galloping quarters. The tail, carried in a graceful curve, is set low. It is thick at the root, tapering to a point.

The Bedlington gives an all-over picture of grace and gentleness, with an underlying feeling of speed and alertness.

# BELGIAN SHEPHERD DOG

*Working group*

**Size**
Males: 61–66 cm (24–26 ins)
Females: 56–61 cm (22–24 ins)

**Coat**
Double-coated, with an extremely dense undercoat and a long, straight, abundant topcoat of medium harshness. It should not be silky or wiry.

**Colour**
There are two varieties of the Belgian Shepherd Dog, and both are growing steadily in popularity. The Groenendael is completely black and the Tervueren may range from red to fawn or mahogany. The face of the Tervueren should have a black mask, which should not extend above the line of the eyes. The ears should be mainly black. The tail should typically have a darker or black tip, and the tips of the light-coloured body hairs should be blackened. Both varieties may have a small white mark on the chest, between pads of the feet and on the tips of the

hind toes, as well as some frosting (white or grey hairs) on the muzzle.

**Grooming**
A good brush and comb keeps the coat in perfect condition.

**Exercise**
Belgian Shepherd Dogs enjoy exercise, especially a good romp in the park.

**Temperament**
These dogs are courageous, affectionate and vigilant. They are somewhat wary of strangers but should be neither nervous and timid, or overly aggressive.

**Suitability as a family companion**
Growing in popularity, Belgian Shepherd Dogs are proving intelligent, adaptable family dogs for either town or country.

This medium-sized breed is one of several varieties of shepherd dogs. They were rather haphazardly bred in various regions of Belgium in the past, but have more recently become quite distinctive in type and excellent in temperament.

The head is long, with a skull of medium width and a flattened rather than a rounded forehead. The eyes are slightly almond-shaped and preferably dark.

The erect ears have a distinctive, triangular appearance and are set high. The body should be powerful and the chest deep and low, giving plenty of heart and lung room. The back is straight and muscular.

The front legs are strongly boned, with wiry and powerful muscle structure and the hindquarters should also be well muscled and powerful. The tail is of medium length and at no time should be lifted above the line of the back. The movement is brisk and free, covering plenty of ground. The front feet are round, with arched toes close together and good, thick, springy soles, while the hind feet are similar, but oval.

# BERNESE MOUNTAIN DOG

*Working group*

**Size**
Males: 66–68 cm (26–26.75 ins)
Females: 60–63 cm (23.5–25 ins)

**Coat**
Soft and silky, with a bright natural sheen. It is long and wavy when mature, but should not curl.

**Colour**
Jet black with rich reddish brown on the cheeks, over the eyes, on all four legs and on the chest. There is a small medium-sized symmetrical white blaze on the head, and white chest marking (called the *cross*) are essential. Preferred, but not essential, are white paws, with the white not reaching higher than the pasterns and a white tip to the tail.

**Grooming**
The coat is easy to manage, and just needs a regular brush and comb.

**Exercise**
For their size and weight, these are extremely active and agile dogs. They need a fair amount of exercise, which they enjoy to the full.

**Temperament**
Intelligent, courageous and faithful.

**Suitability as a family companion**
This is a delightful breed, a fine family pet: understanding and docile with children.

The Bernese Mountain Dog was developed as a cattle and general purpose dog in Switzerland. Over the years it has proved an excellent all round working dog and a dependable guard. It is amenable to training and eager to work.

Its colouring is quite striking. The head is short and massive, with a flat skull, having a well defined stop and slight furrow. The eyes are dark brown and almond-shaped, and the ears are flat in repose. The body is strong and powerful in every respect with a good deep brisket and broad chest. The back is straight and firm, the hindquarters strong, broad and well muscled, and the feet short, round and compact. The bushy tail reaches to just below the hocks, and it should not be carried over the back.

# BICHON FRISE

*Toy group*

**Size**
Males and females: 22.5–27.5 cm (9–11
ins)

**Coat**
Fine, silky with soft corkscrew curls,
neither flat nor corded if left
untrimmed.

**Colour**
Pure white.

**Grooming**
The Bichon is a breed that really needs
good grooming and daily care.
Scissored into shape to give the powder-
puff look, it also requires frequent
combing to keep the tangles away, and
a regular bath.

**Exercise**
An active little dog, the Bichon enjoys
going out and about. It is ideal in either
town or country.

**Temperament**
Gay and happy.

**Suitability as a family companion**
This sturdy and lively little breed has a
delightful temperament. It does not
shed its coat. Providing one is prepared
to spend the time on keeping it well
groomed, its needs are simple and in
return it will prove an enchanting
companion.

**Special needs**
It is important to keep the hair at the
inside corners of the eyes short and also
to clean the eyes daily, as they can get
discoloured here if not attended to. The
inside of the ears must be kept clean
and wax-free.

Developed in France from the Maltese,
this delightful breed is gaining many
followers.

As with many toy breeds, the
Bichon's head is an important feature.
It should be carried proud and high.
The skull is longer than the muzzle and
rather flat, although the hair tends to
make it look round. The cheeks are flat.

Pigment is important: the nose should
be black, round and shiny. The eyes are
dark and vivacious, with dark eye-rims.
The ears should hang close to the head
and well covered with hair. The legs
should be straight and the chest well
developed. The hindquarters are broad
and well rounded, the feet are tight and
small, with the nails preferably black.

The tail is low-set and carried high. It
is gracefully curved, with the hair
always falling into the back. It should
not be tightly curled, nor should it
touch the backbone.

Growing in popularity, the Bichon is
a toy breed that fits happily and well
into modern life.

# BLOODHOUND

*Hound group*

**Size**
Males: 63–69 cm (25–27 ins) 41 kg (90 lbs)
Females: 58–63 cm (23–25 ins) 36 kg (80 lbs)

**Coat**
Short and fairly hard.

**Colour**
Black-and-tan, liver-and-tan or red. A small amount of white is permissible on the chest, feet, and tip of stern.

**Grooming**
Give this dog a good rub over with the hound glove. Pay attention to keeping the eyes clean.

**Exercise**
It requires a lot of exercise.

**Temperament**
Affectionate, though somewhat reserved and sensitive.

**Suitability as a family companion**
This is a breed for an understanding owner. It is a one-person dog rather than a family pet.

**Special needs**
Be guided by the advice the dog's breeder gives you on feeding, general care and welfare. The wrinkling on the head means eyes can sometimes be something of a problem. Avoid a puppy with any signs of eye discharge or excessive wrinkle.

Credited with splendid powers as a tracker, Bloodhounds were developed long ago by the monks of Saint Hubert's monastery in France. It is not clear how they came to get their name.

The Bloodhound's skin is extremely loose: especially around the head and neck, where it hangs in deep folds.

The head is narrow and the nostrils, as one would expect, should be large and open. The eyes are deeply sunk and the ears are extremely long. They hang in folds, the lower parts curling inwards.

The chest is well let down between the forelegs. The hindquarters are muscular and the tail is long and thick, tapering and carried scimitar-fashion. The movement is elastic, swinging and free.

This noble and dignified breed is one of the most placid and gentle of all dogs. It can be quite sensitive: harsh treatment can easily spoil the delightful temperament.

# BORDER COLLIE

*Working group*

**Size**
Males: ideally 53 cm (21 ins)
Females: slightly less

**Coat**
Double coated. The dense, medium-textured topcoat of moderate length and dense short soft undercoat give weather-resisting protection. There is abundant coat to form mane, breeching and brush.

**Colour**
Usually black-and-white or tricolour, although a variety of colours is permissible. The white should not predominate.

**Grooming**
The weather-resisting coat is easy to manage, needing only a regular brush and comb.

**Exercise**
Exercise is important for this active and intelligent dog. It must receive enough, and not be allowed to become bored.

**Temperament**
Lively, loyal and very intelligent.

**Suitability as a family companion**
This is an excellent family pet, providing one accepts the breed was developed first and foremost as a working dog, and as such enjoys an active life. It is responsive to training.

**Special needs**
Its herding instinct is strong, so a safe, fenced garden is essential.

The Collie is a working dog, full of grace and quality. The skull is fairly broad and the muzzle should be moderately short and strong: the skull and foreface being approximately the same length. The nose should be black and the nostrils well developed. The expression should be mild, yet keen, alert and intelligent. The eyes should be wide apart, oval and dark brown, except in the case of blue merles. In these, one or both eyes, or part of one or both, may be blue. The ears should be semi-erect and of medium size. The body should be moderately long and the back broad and strong.

The hindquarters are broad and muscular and the tail is fairly long. The movement should be free, smooth and tireless, with a minimum of lift, giving the impression of an ability to move with great stealth.

# BORDER TERRIER

*Terrier group*

**Size**
Males: 6–7 kg (13–15.5 lbs)
Females: 5.2–6.3 kg (11.5–14 lbs)

**Coat**
Harsh and dense, with a close undercoat. The skin must be thick.

**Colour**
Red, wheaten, grizzle and tan, or blue and tan.

**Grooming**
The coat needs only a regular brush and comb, and just enough trimming to keep in shape.

**Exercise**
This dog enjoys as much exercise as you care to give it. It can adapt equally well to a town or country life style.

**Temperament**
A quiet and sociable terrier.

**Suitability as a family companion**
The most unspoilt of all the terrier breeds, the Border makes an excellent house dog and family companion. It is good with children.

**Special needs**
It can be inclined to go off on hunting trips, so make sure your garden is well fenced.

This hardy, sporting terrier originated in the English-Scottish border area – hence its name. Its origins as a dog that worked with hounds have ensured a sensible and sociable temperament as well as gameness and activity.

The head should be like that of an otter, with a moderately broad skull and a strong, short muzzle. The eyes are dark, with a keen expression. The small ears are of moderate thickness, 'V'-shaped and dropping forward. The body is deep, narrow and fairly long and it should be possible to get both your hands around the part of the body just behind the shoulders. The hindquarters are racy and the loin strong. The tail is moderately short and fairly thick. It should be carried gaily, but not curled over the back.

Although the breed is built on racy lines, this does not mean one should accept weediness in a puppy.

# BORZOI

*Hound group*

**Size**
Males: 74 cm (29 ins) or more
Females: 68 cm (27 ins) or more

**Coat**
Long and silky, certainly not woolly,
flat or wavy. There should be a profuse,
rather curly frill on the neck. The
forelegs and chest are well feathered,
with long and profuse feathering on the
hindquarters and tail.

**Colour**
All colours are allowed.

**Grooming**
Regular grooming with a brush and
comb will help keep the coat in good
condition.

**Exercise**
A lot of free exercise is a must if this
breed is to be kept in good, hard
condition.

**Temperament**
Gentle and reserved. Its aloofness
should not be mistaken for shyness. Do
not choose a puppy that is timid.

**Suitability as a family companion**
This graceful, aristocratic breed needs
understanding to get the best out of it.
It will not readily enjoy the company of
children and their games and activities.

Borzois, like all Greyhounds, are of
very ancient origin. They were bred in
Russia, first to protect people against
wolves and later, when wolf-hunting
became popular, as hunting dogs.

The Borzoi is very elegant and
posesses great speed, courage and
muscular power. The head should be
long and lean, converging very
gradually to the tip of the nose. The
eyes are almond-shaped: dark, alert,
intelligent and keen. The ears lie back,
close to the head.

The back rises in a graceful arch from
as near the shoulders as possible, while
the hindquarters are broad and
powerful. The front feet are rather long,
with the toes close together. The hind
feet are longer and less arched. The tail
is long, set on low and well feathered.

The elegant Borzoi can be a clean,
affectionate and graceful companion,
but does need plenty of exercise.

# BOSTON TERRIER

*Utility group*

**Size**
Males and females: no more than 11.4 kg (25 lbs)

**Coat**
Short, smooth, bright and fine in texture.

**Colour**
Brindle with white markings is preferred, although black with white markings is permissible. The ideal markings are a white muzzle, an even white blaze over the head, collar, breast, part or whole of the forelegs and on the hindings below the hock.

**Grooming**
The short coat requires only a regular brush and then a rub over with a cloth.

**Exercise**
This dog is not at all demanding in its exercise needs. A walk on the lead or a free run in the garden is usually quite sufficient.

**Temperament**
Highly intelligent, lively and affectionate.

**Suitability as a family companion**
This smart, adaptable little breed is especially suitable for the not-so-young, as it fits in well with flat life or restricted living. It can be somewhat lazy, but it can also be a lively dog, quite suitable for the average family.

**Special needs**
Except for needing attention to the nails, ears and eyes, this is not a demanding breed.

As its name implies, the Boston Terrier originated in the United States. It is smart and eye-catching, with attractive markings, clean lines and a short coat.

It should be a well-balanced, stylish dog. The head is a most important feature; the skull should be square, and the muzzle short, square and free from wrinkle. The stop is well defined, and the jaws broad and square with chops of good depth but not pendulous. The eyes are wide apart, large, round and dark, giving an alert, but kind expression. They should be set square to the skull. The erect ears are small and thin, and set as near the corner of the skull as possible.

The Boston has a deep, short, body with a good width of chest. It should not appear chunky. The feet should be round, small and compact, the tail is set on low and is short, fine and tapering, either straight or screw.

# BOXER

*Working group*

**Size**
Males: 56–61 cm (22–24 ins) 30 kg (66 lbs)
Females: 53–58 cm (21–23 ins) 28 kg (62 lbs)

**Coat**
Short and shiny, smooth and lying close to the body.

**Colour**
Fawn, brindle, or red in various shades, with white markings, which should not exceed one-third of the ground colour. White Boxers are not accepted in the show ring.

**Grooming**
The short coat requires a good rub with the hound glove to keep it healthy and in good order. With this breed, coat shedding is minimal.

**Exercise**
The boxer needs a good-sized garden and will enjoy a romp in the park. It is not a breed that should be walked off its feet, but it enjoys being active.

**Temperament**
Docile, but distrustful of strangers. It needs kind but firm handling.

**Suitability as a family companion**
The clean-limbed, faithful Boxer has a great love for its owner and household. With its cheerful disposition, it makes a splendid and companionable pet. It is not among the longest-living breeds.

**Special needs**
Boxers like to join in all the family activities, and also appreciate routine.

This is a medium-sized, sturdy breed. It originated in Germany and first came to notice after World War II.

The head is of great importance. The muzzle should be broad and deep, with a good chin and a well-padded lip. There should be a distinctive stop. The mouth is undershot, with powerful teeth and well developed cheeks. A black mask is essential, though white may sometimes stretch over the muzzle. The eyes should be dark brown.

The Boxer should have a deep chest and straight well boned legs. The whole back should be short, straight, broad and muscular. The hindquarters are strong, and the feet should be small with tightly arched toes and hard soles. The tail is carried high and is customarily docked. The Boxer's movement is alive with energy.

Tolerant with children, the Boxer is a breed that develops to its full with human companionship.

# BRIARD

*Working group*

**Size**
Males: 61–69 cm (24–27 ins)
Females: 58–64 cm (23–25.5 ins)

**Coat**
The topcoat should be long on the body: not less than 7 cm (3 ins), slightly wavy, with a crisp texture. The undercoat is fine and dense.

**Colour**
All black, slate grey or all shades of fawn. The darker shades are preferred. Fawns may have dark shadings on the ears, muzzle, back and tail, but it is important that these blend into the rest of the coat.

**Grooming**
Regular grooming is essential. Give the dog a good brush and comb, right down to the skin.

**Exercise**
The energetic Briard needs plenty of exercise and the opportunity for a good run.

**Temperament**
Quiet, gentle and solid. Choose a puppy that is friendly, with no trace of timidity or shyness.

**Suitability as a family companion**
The Briard does not shed, though its undercoat loosens. It does not, however, come out on the furniture, carpet or clothing. The dog adapts easily to home conditions, is good with children and is tolerant of their playfulness and teasing. Its acute sense of hearing and good deep bark makes it an excellent watch-dog.

The Briard is an old French breed: a long-haired sheep and cattle dog which has changed little in appearance or character over hundreds of years.
It is intelligent, lively, and well proportioned. The head is large and the skull slightly rounded, with a square, strong muzzle. The nose is large and always black. The hair around the muzzle forms a moustache and a beard. Above the eyebrows, it forms a light veil, covering the large, dark brown eyes. The ears are covered with long hair and are placed high.
The Briard should be slightly longer in the body than it is high at the shoulder. The back is level, the chest broad and the forelegs and hind legs are both well muscled. There are double dew-claws on the hind legs. The feet should be strong, slightly rounded and have firm, hard pads.
The tail is long and well covered with hair. It is carried low and should have an upward hook at the tip.

# BULLDOG

*Utility group*

**Size**
Males: ideally, about 25 kg (55 lbs)
Females: ideally, about 22.7 kg (50 lbs)

**Coat**
Fine in texture, short close and smooth. Its hardness is due only to its closeness and shortness.

**Colour**
Whole colours, smut (which is a whole colour with a black mask or muzzle) or pied (which is a combination of white with any of the whole colours). The preferred whole colours and their varieties are red, brindle, fawn and white.

**Grooming**
A regular good brush will keep the short coat in order, but the face wrinkles will require attention from time to time to keep them clean and dry. A little petroleum jelly on the nose will stop it from cracking.

**Exercise**
Although it is not inclined to exercise, the Bulldog enjoys a good walk and the chance of a good run.

**Temperament**
Affectionate, docile and dignified.

**Suitability as a family companion**
A real character, the Bulldog is beautiful in its ugliness. It is a great family dog excellent with children. A breed that has been much maligned, it has a good life expectancy and can be surprisingly active. Its formidable appearance with its suggestion of great strength and courage belies a docile and affectionate, though somewhat obstinate nature.

**Special needs**
Its owners need to be patient with it, as it prefers to please itself rather than anyone else.

The Bulldog is of British origin. It has a large head with a flat foreface, rounded cheeks and wrinkled, loose skin about the face. The muzzle should be short, broad and very deep. The nose is broad and black. The jaws are massive and square with the lower one projecting. The flews should be thick and hang over the bottom jaw.

The eyes are set wide apart and are dark and round. The small, thin ears are the type known as 'rose', folding inwards at the back while the upper and front edges curve out and back. The front legs are muscular and short in proportion to the hind legs. The feet are round and compact, with the forefeet turning slightly outwards. The tail has a thick root and a fine tip. It should hang low, straight or screwed.

The Bulldog has a peculiar, constrained movement and seems to walk with its right shoulder rather advanced and with short, quick steps on the tips of its toes.

It is a great character: faithful and friendly with an excellent temperament.

# BULLMASTIFF

*Working group*

**Size**
Males: 63.5–68.5 cm (25–27 ins) 50–59 kg (110–130 lbs)
Females: 61–66 cm (24–26 ins) 41–50 kg (90–110 lbs)
With this breed, the height must be in proportion to the weight and soundness.

**Coat**
Short and hard giving good weather protection. The coat should lie flat to the body; any tendency to woolliness or silkiness is completely wrong.

**Colour**
Any shade of brindle, fawn or red, but the colour must be pure and clear. A dark muzzle is essential.

**Grooming**
The short coat needs little attention. A good brushing, especially when moulting, will be fine.

**Exercise**
It needs sensible exercise to keep it in good shape, but there is no need to overdo it.

**Temperament**
Good-tempered, affectionate and reliable.

**Suitability as a family companion**
For those looking for a sizeable, clean-limbed dog that is powerful, intelligent and good with its own family and children, this breed fits the bill. It is a reliable guard and will deter any unwelcome visitors.

**Special needs**
It has quite a big frame and the puppy has plenty of growing to do. Feed it sensibly and well, and do not over-exercise it. When fully grown, make sure you do not overfeed and under-exercise the dog, as it will become fat, ungainly and lethargic.

The Bullmastiff was developed in Britain within the last hundred years and has the Bulldog and English Mastiff as its forebears.

This is a powerfully built dog. The head is large and square with a wrinkle when the dog is interested. The stop is definite and the muzzle short, broad under the eyes, blunt and with a broad under-jaw and nose. A dark mask is desirable, as are medium-sized dark or hazel eyes. The ears are short and 'V'-shaped or folded back. They are set on wide and high, making the skull look square, and are a deeper colour than the body.

The neck should be arched and muscular, and the chest deep and wide. The back should be short and straight and the hindquarters are strong and muscular, slightly rounded over the rump. The feet are round and tight, with good hard pads. The tail reaches the hocks, strong at the root and tapering.

The Bullmastiff is eager to learn and to please, and it also makes a good guard dog that is completely happy and safe within the family circle.

# BULL TERRIER

*Terrier group*

## Size
This breed comes in two sizes, Standard and Miniature:
*Standard*: there are neither height nor weight limits with this breed, but there should be the impression of the maximum substance in proportion to the size of the dog.
*Miniature*: no more than 35 cm (14 ins)

## Coat
Short, flat, even and harsh to the touch, with a fine gloss. The skin should fit the dog tightly.

## Colour
Either white or coloured. The white should be a pure white though markings on the head are permissible. With the coloureds (which should predominate) the breed has a variety of colours – all brindles, black-brindle, tricolour, red, red-smut, fawn and fawn-smut.

## Grooming
A good brushing after exercise is all that is required.

## Exercise
This breed will take as much exercise as it is given.

## Temperament
Full of fire and courage and with a great sense of humour, Bull Terriers are even-tempered and amenable to discipline.

## Suitability as a family companion
This breed is an excellent housedog. It is a strong protector of family and property and can also be long-suffering as a friend to children – so long as they respect its needs.

## Special needs
A Bull Terrier needs to be taught its place with kindness and understanding.

The original Bull Terrier was bred for bull-baiting and dog fighting. Today, the breed is game, with a Bulldog's tenacity and the Terrier's spirit.

It is the gladiator of the canine race: strongly built, muscular and active. The head should be strong, long and deep, but not coarse. From the front, it should appear egg-shaped, with no hollows or indentations. The underjaw is strong. The eyes look narrow and sunken. They should be black, or as dark as possible, with a piercing glint. The ears should be small, neat and placed close together. The body is firm, muscular and well rounded. The neck should be muscular, long and arched. The feet should be round and compact. The tail is short and set low, thick at the root, tapering to a fine point.

The Bull Terrier is an ideal country dog, but is not suitable for town life unless it is able to have good, free exercise daily.

The Bull Terrier (Miniature) is an exact replica of its larger cousin except for the height restriction. Short-backed with excellent bone, it is a big dog with a small frame.

# CAIRN TERRIER

*Terrier group*

**Size**
Males and females: ideally 6.3 kg (14 lbs)

**Coat**
A correct coat is very important: it must be double-coated with a profuse, hard (but not coarse) outer coat and a short, soft, close undercoat.

**Colour**
Red, sandy, grey-brindle or nearly black. Darker points are typical, especially on the muzzle and ears.

**Grooming**
This coat needs regular brushing and combing to remove dead hairs.

**Exercise**
It is quite content to exercise within the house and garden.

**Temperament**
Fearless, with a gay disposition.

**Suitability as a family companion**
A Cairn enjoys playing with children. It is a faithful and gay family dog.

This sporting terrier is the most ancient of all the Scottish breeds. Active and game, it enjoys great popularity. Its name comes from its use as a killer of foxes and vermin in the 'cairns' (rocky crags) of Scotland.

The distinctive shaggy appearance and perky expression hold great appeal. The head is small, but in proportion to the body, with a somewhat foxy appearance. It should be well covered with hair. The ears are small, pointed and carried erect. The eyes are dark and set wide apart.

The body is compact, with a straight back and strong hindquarters. The tail is carried gaily and is well covered with hair, though not feathery. The movement should be very free.

The tough and natural Cairn is a most affectionate and faithful companion.

# CHIHUAHUA (Smooth and Long Coated)

*Toy group*

**Size**
Males and females: preferably 0.9–1.8 kg (2–4 lbs): no more than 2.7 kg (6 lbs).

**Coat**
*Smooth:* soft-textured, close and glossy. *Long:* soft (never coarse or harsh to the touch) either flat or slightly wavy, and not a tight, curly coat. There should be feathering on the legs and hindquarters. A large ruff on the neck is desirable and preferred. The tail should be a long, full plume. The ears are fringed.

**Colour**
Any colour, or mixture of colours, is acceptable.

**Grooming**
The long-coated variety needs a certain amount of brushing and combing. The smooth-coated ones needs only a rub over with a cloth or a brush.

**Exercise**
They will exercise themselves within the home, flat or small garden.

**Temperament**
Bold and saucy.

**Suitability as a family companion**
These game little dogs prove most intelligent and suitable for anyone for whom exercising may be something of a problem.

**Special needs**
Keep an eye on the teeth, and keep the nails cut short.

Chihuahuas originated in Mexico. They are sharp, alert little dogs, relatively strong and robust for their size. They can be good burglar alarms, as they are courageous and always interested in everything that is going on.

The Chihuahua is a small, dainty and compact dog, with a brisk, forceful action. It should have a round, apple-head with fine cheeks and an accentuated stop.

The jaws are lean and the nose is moderately short. The ears are large and set at an angle of about 45 degrees, giving breadth between them. The eyes are brilliant, full, round and set well apart. The body is compact, and slightly tucked-up giving a graceful appearance. The ribs are well sprung with a deep brisket. The back is straight and the feet should be dainty. The tail is of medium length carried up or over the back. It is flattish in appearance, broadening slightly in the centre and tapering to a point.

Small as it is, the Chihuahua is a loyal and devoted friend to its owner and family.

# CHINESE CRESTED

*Toy group*

**Size**
Males and females: 3.2–5.4 kg (7–12 lbs)

**Coat**
Smooth, with hair on the neck, feet and tail only. Those with an all-over coat, which can be either somewhat sparse or full, are known as 'Powder Puffs'.

**Colour**
Any colour, plain or spotted.

**Grooming**
The hairless type needs a bath from time to time, and a light rub over the skin with baby oil afterwards is beneficial. The Powder Puffs need a regular brush and comb and occasional bath.

**Exercise**
Although dainty and gentle, this breed is surprisingly active and thoroughly enjoys exercise. It makes a splendid sight when on the move with its mane and plume flying in the wind.

**Temperament**
Somewhat aloof with strangers, but this should not be mistaken for shyness. It is intelligent, courageous and loyal but can be a little wilful.

**Suitability as a family companion**
Clean, odourless and very affectionate, these dogs make splendid if unusual family pets. They are also excellent as watchdogs, but are not noisy or yappy.

**Special needs**
Surprisingly perhaps, this is a hardy breed and despite its nakedness it can easily cope with and adjust to climate changes. It needs no special skin treatment.

This breed probably originated thousands of years ago, but no one is quite certain exactly when or where. No one even seems to know how it got its name.

It is a small, active and graceful dog, somewhat houndish with medium to fine bones and smooth, soft skin. The head is wedge-shaped with a slightly rounded skull. The eyes are moderately dark, round and set wide apart. The ears are large and erect. The body is medium to long, and the chest is fairly broad and deep.

The tail is carried over the back or looped. There is a mane or crest, which can be flat, or long and flowing, profuse or sparse.

The ears may or may not have fringing, and the legs have furnishings which should not extend above the knee on the forelegs or above the hock on the hindlegs. The last two-thirds of the tail is also plumed.

Despite appearances, this is a robust, adaptable dog that enjoys an active life. It is also extremely loving.

# CHOW

*Utility group*

**Size**
Males and females: at least 45.7 cm (18 ins)

**Coat**
Abundant, dense, straight and stand-off. The outer coat is rather coarse in texture, while the undercoat is soft and woolly.

**Colour**
Whole-coloured in black, red, blue, fawn, cream or white. Frequently shaded but not in patches or part-coloured. The underpart of the tail and back of the thighs are frequently of a lighter colour.

**Grooming**
A twice weekly thorough grooming and daily brush is important, especially when the dog is moulting.

**Exercise**
The Chow is basically quite lazy, but nevertheless enjoys a good walk and romp.

**Temperament**
The Chow is independent and enjoys a routine. It is at its best within the family, to whom it is completely loyal.

**Suitability as a family companion**
The Chow is a one-family dog, nice with children and aloof with strangers. It is not aggressive with other dogs, and is a good watch-dog.

**Special needs**
Follow the breeder's recommendations for feeding your puppy.

The Chow is an active dog, well balanced and with a proud and dignified bearing, almost leonine in appearance.

The skull is flat and broad, the muzzle is moderate in length, with an indentation rather than a pronounced stop. The nose is black, with large, wide nostrils. The ears are small, thick, and upright, carried well forward and set wide apart. The eyes should be dark, small and almond-shaped, giving the breed its characteristic scowl. It is unique in having a bluish-black tongue, mouth and gums.

The chest is broad and deep and the back straight and strong. The hind legs are muscular and the hocks straight, giving a stilted movement. The feet are small, round and cat-like and the tail is set high and carried well over the back.

This dog is especially delightful as a puppy, when it looks like a teddy bear. It is one of the most individual of breeds.

# COLLIE (Rough and Smooth)

*Working group*

**Size**
Males: 56–61 cm (22–24 ins) 20.4–29.5 kg (45–65 lbs)
Females: 51–56 cm (20–22 ins) 18–25 kg (40–55 lbs)

**Coat**
*Roughs:* The coat should fit the outline of the dog and be very dense. The outercoat is straight and harsh to the touch. The undercoat is furry, soft and very close. The mane, and frill should be very abundant, the forelegs well feathered and the hind legs above the hock profusely so, but smooth below. The tail is profusely feathered.
*Smooths:* the topcoat is short, flat and harsh in texture, with a very dense undercoat.

**Colour**
There are three recognized colours. Sables are any shade from light gold to rich mahogany, or shaded sable. Tricolours are predominantly black with rich tan markings about the head and legs.
Blue merles are predominantly clear silvery-blue, splashed and marbled with black. Rich tan markings are preferred, but their absence is not a fault.
All the above may carry the typical white collie markings. A blaze may be carried on the muzzle or skull or both.

A fully or partly white collar, a white shirt, legs and feet and a white tip to the tail are favoured.

**Grooming**
The characteristic coat of the Roughs is not difficult to keep well groomed. A good deep-down brush with a bristle brush once or twice a week and a daily brush and comb when the dog is moulting will keep the coat in fine condition and free of tangles.
The Smooths have no real grooming problems. Their short, weather-resisting coat with its short moulting period needs only a good weekly brush and comb.

**Exercise**
Collies enjoy a really good walk and run in the park or in the country.

**Temperament**
These dogs are gentle and sweet-natured, but somewhat aloof with strangers.

**Suitability as a family companion**
The Collie enjoys companionship and is good with children. It is content within its own confines and makes an ideal companion.

**Special needs**
It should not be allowed to get bored, as it can be noisy and destructive.

The Collie is a delightful outdoor dog, and easy to train. It is attractive in both its forms, with a smooth, wedge-shaped head. The skull is flat and should be of equal length to the foreface. The eyes should be medium-sized, almond-shaped and brown, except in the blue merles, when one or both eyes may be wall or blue-flecked. It has an intelligent, alert expression.
With the Roughs, the ears are small, but in the Smooths they should be moderately large and wide at the base. They are brought forward when the dog is alert and carried semi-erect, with the top third tipping forward.
The body is long, the back firm and the chest deep. Its movement is quite distinctive, with the front feet close together and the hindlegs powerful and full of drive. It should have a long stride that seems light and effortless. The tail is long, reaching the hock, and the hair is profuse.

# DACHSHUND

*Hound group*

**Size**
There are six varieties, three Standard and three Miniature:
*Standard smooth:*
Males: no more than 11.3 kg (25 lbs)
Females: no more than 10.4 kg (23 lbs)
*Standard longhaired:*
Males and females: around 7.7–8.2 kg (17–18 lbs), but can be a little more.
*Standard wirehaired:*
Males: 9–10 kg (20–22 lbs)
Females: 8.2–9 kg (18–20 lbs)

*Miniatures:* these can also be smooth, longhaired or wirehaired. In all varieties, the weight of both male and female should be no more than 5 kg (11 lbs), ideally 4.5 kg (10 lbs).

**Coat**
*Smooth*: short, dense and strong. The skin should be loose and supple, but close-fitting all over, without much wrinkle.
*Longhaireds*: soft and straight or only slightly waved. There is longer hair under the neck, behind the legs and the underparts of the body, with an abundance of feathering on the hindquarters and on the tail, where is should form a flag. The outside of the ears are also well feathered. The coat should be flat.
*Wirehaireds*: short and harsh, with an undercoat. The hair on the ears is almost smooth. There should be a beard on the chin and the eyebrows are bushy.

**Grooming**
All three coats are easy to cope with. The sleek Smooths need a good going over with a hound glove, the glamorous Longs need a regular brush and comb, and the Wires need stripping about twice a year as well as regular combing.

**Exercise**
Dachshunds are most adaptable, and not at all demanding. They enjoy a country life, and, if they live in a town, they should have plenty of walks and a chance to run in the park.

**Suitability as a family companion**
A Dachshund is a strong-minded dog, but it is an excellent companion and good with children. Miniatures especially are suitable for those who are elderly, or who have limited space. All types have a good life expectancy.

**Special needs**
Dachshunds can be lazy. It is important to make sure yours get enough exercise. They can also be vocal, and should be trained to get rid of this tendency.

The Dachshund was used for hunting in burrows for foxes and badgers. Its loose but well fitting skin enables it to manoeuvre easily underground. It has a keen sense of smell and a deep baying voice.

It is bold and will force its way through dense cover. Low to the ground, the Dachshund is sturdily-built and well muscled. It should not be clumsy or restricted in movement. The head, which should be carried boldy, looks long. The eyes are medium-sized, set obliquely and usually dark. In the chocolate or dapples, one or both wall eyes are permissible.

The ears are broad, moderately long, well rounded and very mobile. The body is long and muscular. The tail is set on fairly high, strong and tapering. The chest should have ample heart room and the breast bone is very prominent.

This lively and versatile breed was bred to work, and has proved itself an excellent family dog.

# DALMATIAN

*Utility group*

### Size
Males: 58–61 cm (23–24 ins)
Females: 55–58 cm (22–23 cm)
(With this breed, overall balance is of prime importance.)

### Coat
Short, hard and dense, sleek and glossy in appearance.

### Colour
The ground colour should be pure white. Black spotted dogs should have dense black spots, and liver spotted dogs liver-brown spots. The spotting should not run together, but be round and well defined and as well distributed as possible. The spots on the extremities should be smaller than those on the body.

### Grooming
Good regular brushing is essential with this breed, otherwise their hairs will be everywhere.

### Exercise
Dalmatians are active dogs that need ample and free exercise.

### Temperament
This is a sound and friendly dog, loyal and lively.

### Suitability as a family companion
The Dalmatian has a good life expectancy. It is medium-sized, faithful: an admirable companion and family dog which enjoys all family activities.

### Special needs
This dog should not be left on its own for long periods.

The attractive Dalmatian was once used for hunting and in England, at the turn of the century, it was considered very stylish to have a Dalmatian running between the wheels of a carriage.

It is a balanced, strong, muscular dog. With the black-spotted variety, the nose is black. In livers it is brown. The eye rims and eye colour also match the spotting. The eyes are set fairly well apart and should be round, bright and intelligent. The ears are set on high and should be spotted.

The chest should be deep, giving plenty of heart and lung room. The back is level and the loins and hindquarters should be strong. The tail should reach approximately to the hock and is carried with a slight upward curve. It should be strong and tapering. The feet are round, well arched and have tough pads.

# DANDIE DINMONT

*Terrier group*

**Size**
Males and females: 20–28 cm (8–11 ins)
8 kg (18 lbs)

**Coat**
About 5 cm (2 ins) long, a mixture of hardish (but not wiry) and soft hair, giving a crisp feel. The hair on the underbody is lighter in colour and softer than on top. The head is covered with very soft, silky hair. The lighter the colour and the silkier in texture it is, the better.

**Colour**
There are two colours: pepper and mustard. The pepper ranges from a dark blueish-black to a light silvery grey. The mustard ranges from a reddish brown to a pale fawn.

**Grooming**
Regular grooming with a good brush and comb will be sufficient, although a little trimming and shaping of the coat and head will enhance the appearance.

**Exercise**
This dog enjoys plenty of regular exercise, but it will be quite content within an average-sized garden.

**Temperament**
A friendly terrier that can be self-willed and stubborn, as well as affectionate and outgoing.

**Suitability as a family companion**
The Dandie is very loyal to the family and useful as a watchdog, as it has a good, deep bark for its size.

**Special needs**
It does not like to be left alone for long.

The Dandie Dinmont is thought to be based on an old variety of terrier raised by gypsies in southern Scotland. It is named after a character in Sir Walter Scott's novel *Guy Mannering*.

This is a low-to-the-ground terrier, with a strongly made head. The skull is broad and the forehead domed. The rich, dark, hazel eyes are round, bright and expressive.

The ears are pendulous. The body is long, with a well developed chest and well sprung ribs. The forelegs are short and very muscular, set wide apart. The hindlegs are a little longer than the forelegs. The tail is rather short, with a tapering feather. It is carried a little above the level of the back.

The Dandie is keen and intelligent, as well as being a sporting terrier. It makes an excellent companion: hard to resist when it turns to you with its large brown eyes, and smiles.

# DOBERMANN

*Working group*

**Size**
Males: ideally 68.5 cm (27 ins)
Females: ideally 65 cm (25.5 ins)

**Coat**
Smooth, short, hard, thick and close-lying.

**Colour**
Black, brown or blue, with rust red markings. These must be sharply defined, and should appear above each eye and on the muzzle, throat and forechest as well as on all the legs and feet, and below the tail.

**Grooming**
A regular, good brush with a hound glove is fine.

**Exercise**
This dog needs a lot of exercise.

**Temperament**
The Dobermann is energetic, determined, bold and intelligent.

**Suitability as a family companion**
This upstanding breed makes a splendid family dog and guard. It is a good playmate for children.

**Special needs**
A Dobermann needs firm handling, especially when it is young.

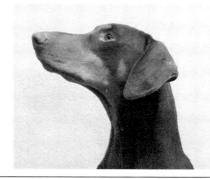

This German breed takes its name from its original breeder, Louis Dobermann. It has a powerful, compact body, a clean-cut appearance, and a fearless expression. All this, combined with a proud carriage, make it an impressive dog.

The long, wedge-shaped head should be in proportion to the body. The almond-shaped eyes have a vigorous, energetic expression. The small, neat ears are set high. The neck is carried erect and should be fairly long and lean. The body is square, with a short, firm back and deep well sprung ribs.

The hindquarters should be well developed and muscular, and the feet tight and cat-like. The movement is balanced and vigorous, with a good reach in front and a strong drive in the hindquarters. The tail, customarily docked, is carried high.

The Dobermann well repays the firmness that it sometimes needs when it is young.

# ELKHOUND

*Hound group*

**Size**
Males: 52 cm (20.5 ins) 23 kg (50 lbs)
Females: 49 cm (19.5 ins) 20 kg (43 lbs)

**Coat**
The topcoat is thick, abundant, coarse and weather-resisting. The undercoat is soft and woolly.

**Colour**
Grey, of various shades with black tips to the long outercoat, lighter on the chest, stomach, legs and the underside of the tail.

**Grooming**
Regular brushing is a must to keep this dog's weather-resisting coat in good order.

**Exercise**
It needs sensible and regular exercise, as this is a hunting breed.

**Temperament**
Good-tempered, determined, highly intelligent.

**Suitability as a family companion**
This is a good pet for the right family, but it requires firm, kind and understanding handling.

**Special needs**
Remember that this breed hunted the elk, which is much heavier and larger than a deer. It was trained to bark on contact and to keep the quarry at bay until the arrival of the hunter. Firmness is needed to prevent the barking habit forming. The breed also has a tendency to put on weight if it is not given plenty of exercise.

A handsome, strong, hardy breed, the Elkhound is remarkably healthy.

The head is broad between the ears, and the muzzle moderately long, with a strong jaw. The eyes should be brown and as dark as possible to give a fearless and friendly expression. The ears are upstanding, pointed and set high. They are expressive and very mobile. The Elkhound is heavy for its size and should have good bone. The chest is wide and deep, the back firm and the tail set high and tightly curled (often with a double curl).

An appealing grey 'teddy bear', the Elkhound puppy needs understanding and firmness if it is to grow up into a well behaved adult.

# ENGLISH SETTER

*Gundog group*

**Size**
Males: 64–67.5 cm (25.5–27 ins) 27–29.7 kg (60–66 lbs)
Females: 60–64 cm (24–25.5 ins) 25.2–29.9 kg (56–62 lbs)

**Coat**
Slightly wavy, long and silky: the tail, breeches and forelegs should be well feathered.

**Colour**
Black-and-white, liver-and-white or tricolour (black, white and tan), all without heavy patches of colour on the body. Preferably, it should be flecked all over.

**Grooming**
It needs regular brushing and combing and the occasional bath. The hair should be shortened on the ears and under the throat.

**Exercise**
The Setter is more suited to the country than to town life. An owner must be prepared to give the dog enough exercise.

**Temperament**
Gentle and affectionate, with a most amiable disposition.

**Suitability as a family companion**
Setters thrive on human company and are ideal companions in the right home.

The English setter is one of the most beautiful breeds, full of grace and elegance. It is of medium height and clean in outline, with a reasonably long head. The stop is definite, and there is plenty of brain room. The muzzle is moderately deep and fairly square. The nose colour should be black or liver according to the body colour. The eyes should be dark hazel (the darker the better) bright and intelligent with a sweet, melting expression. The ears are of moderate length, set low and hanging in neat folds. The neck is long and lean.

The body is well built and deep, with strong hindquarters. The tail is slightly curved, but with no tendency to turn upwards. It should be set almost in line with the back and be of medium length.

This breed takes time to mature and the dog is often boisterous until it is 18 months or two years old.

# ENGLISH TOY TERRIER

*Toy group*

**Size**
Males and females: ideally 25.5–30.5 cm
(10–12 ins) 2.7–3.6 kg (6–8 lbs)

**Coat**
A thick, close, smooth and glossy coat
is required. It should not be sparse.

**Colour**
Black-and-tan. The black should be
ebony, and the tan rich, like a new
chestnut. The colours should not run or
blend into each other but should have
clear lines of colour division. With this
breed it is important that the markings
follow the set pattern and are clearly
defined.

**Grooming**
This dog has an easy-to-keep coat. All
that is needed is a brush and wipe over
with a cloth.

**Exercise**
These dogs like their home comforts,
but they are not at all frail and delicate.
They enjoy being active.

**Temperament**
This is a toy dog with a terrier
temperament and character. It should
not be nervous.

**Suitability as a family companion**
Consider this bright, alert small dog if
space and exercise are problems.

**Special needs**
Although this dog enjoys comfort, it
should not be pampered.

This is an old breed, once used for
killing rats. It should be balanced,
cleanly built, and elegant, giving an
appearance of alertness and speed. The
head is wedge-shaped and should have a
slight stop.
  The eyes should be small, very dark,
almond-shaped and sparkling. The ears
should be erect, slightly pointed, close
together and high on the back of the
skull. The chest should be narrow and
deep. The buttocks should be gently
rounded. The tail, which is set on low
and thick at the root, tapers to a point,
and should not reach below the hock.
The feet should be dainty, compact and
well arched.
  This is an affectionate, clean little dog
whose short coat leaves little evidence of
hairs about the place. It lacks neither
courage nor intelligence and is a first-
rate house dog.

# FINNISH SPITZ

*Working group*

## Size
Males: 44–50 cm (17–20 ins) 14–16 kg (31–36 lbs)
Females: 39–45 cm (15.5–18 ins) 10–13 kg (23–29 lbs)

## Coat
The topcoat is straight with coarse, stand-off long hairs. These are longer on the tail and thighs, and also on the neck, where it forms a ruff. The undercoat is dense and woolly.

## Colour
The coat must be red, which can range from a near-gold to a dark chestnut. The undercoat is always lighter than the top coat. It can be cream, but not white.

## Grooming
This dog needs little grooming other than a thorough brushing once a week. It will need more attention when it is moulting. These dogs are very clean.

## Exercise
With their working background, these dogs enjoy plenty of exercise.

## Temperament
Intelligent, lively, equable and loyal.

## Suitability as a family companion
This is a handy-sized dog, healthy and unspoiled. It is good with children and a sharp watchdog.

## Special needs
It is inquisitive as a young puppy, so the garden needs to be well fenced. It also likes the sound of its own voice, so you will have to be firm about this.

The Finnish Spitz, sometimes known as the 'Finkie', is a good all-round dog originally used as a hunter. It is quick to learn, but it gets bored if made to do the same thing over and over again.

The dog is considerably larger than the bitch and carries more coat. The head is wedge-shaped with a pronounced stop and a pitch-black nose. The almond-shaped eyes are dark and lively, set slanting slightly upwards. The ears are small, crooked and pointed. The back is strong and straight and the chest is deep.

The plumed tail curls immediately from the root and continues in a tight curl (though not a full circle), which lies along the thigh. The dog's movement should be light and springy.

Small enough to live in a modern house, the Finnish Spitz has the personality of a larger dog.

# FOX TERRIER (Wire and Smooth)

*Terrier group*

**Size**
Males: no more than 39 cm (15.5 ins) 8 kg (18 lbs)
Females: slightly smaller, and weighing about 0.9 kg (2 lbs) less

**Coat**
*Smooths*: straight, flat, smooth, hard, dense and abundant.
*Wires*: wiry, dense, with a softer undercoat. Some of the hardest coats are crinkly, or slightly waved, but should never be curly.

**Colour**
White should predominate. Brindle, red, liver on slaty blue are objectionable, but otherwise colour is of no importance.

**Grooming**
*Smooths*: with its close-fitting coat, the Smooth is easy to groom, needing only a good brush and comb to keep it tidy.

*Wires*: these need regular grooming and should be hand-stripped several times a year to retain the coat texture.

**Exercise**
These are busy dogs that will exercise themselves within their own garden and home but, of course, they enjoy a good outing.

**Temperament**
These are gay, brave and loyal little dogs.

**Suitability as a family companion**
They quickly become part of the family and like to participate in everything including children's games. They are at home in the town and in the country.

**Special needs**
This dog has something of a reputation for being yappy and snappy. Sensible management is needed right from the start.

These are tough, handy-sized dogs, originally bred for entering fox earths. They are splendid exterminators of vermin.

The Fox Terrier should be alert and lively, with bone and strength in a small compass. It should look like a cleverly made hunter. The head should be long and lean with a flat skull and a strong jaw. The eyes should be small, dark, rather deep set and full of fire and intelligence. The ears are small and 'V'-shaped and drop forward. The chest should be deep and the hindquarters powerful. The feet are neat, round and compact. The tail is customarily docked and is set on high and carried gaily.

This is an attractive terrier: hardy with a good life expectancy. It enjoys life to the full and is easily trained.

# FRENCH BULLDOG

*Utility group*

**Size**
Males: 12.7 kg (28 lbs)
Females: 10.9 kg (24 lbs)

**Coat**
Smooth, lustrous, of fine texture, short
and close.

**Colour**
Brindle (a mixture of black and
coloured hairs), which may also contain
white, so long as brindle predominates;
pied (when the white predominates over
the brindle); fawns. White dogs are also
classified as pied. The eyelashes and
eyerims should be black. In pieds, the
white should be clear with definite
brindle patches with no ticking or black
spots. Fawns may have brindle hairs,
but must have black eyelashes and
eyerims.

**Grooming**
The French Bulldog needs regular, daily
brushing.

**Exercise**
It will be happy and fit exercising in the
garden, but it enjoys a good walk.

**Temperament**
This is a wonderful character,
affectionate and a great clown with a
lively expression.

**Suitability as a family companion**
It is adaptable and makes a splendid
companion. It loves human company.

**Special needs**
The eyes should be kept clean and the
face folds free of sores. Apply a little
petroleum jelly at times.

The French Bulldog was probably
developed from very small, light dogs of
a Bulldog type which were imported
from France to England by a Mr Krehl
in 1894.

Compactly built and muscular, with
good strong bone, the French Bulldog's
head is massive, broad and square with
a broad deep muzzle and strong, slightly
undershot, lower jaw. The folds and
wrinkles of the skin on the head are
almost symmetrical. The nose is broad
and short, with wide nostrils. The 'bat
ears' are erect and of medium size, wide
at the base, and rounded at the top. The
eyes set wide apart are dark of moderate
size and not sunken or prominent.

The body is muscular and well
rounded. It is wide at the shoulder,
narrowing at the loins. The tail is very
short and set low and either straight or
kinked. It should not curl over the back.

The French Bulldog is a charming
breed, easy to keep as a pet.

# GERMAN SHEPHERD DOG (Alsatian)

*Working group*

### Size
Males: ideally 61–66 cm (24–26 ins)
Females: ideally 56–61 cm (22–24 ins)

### Coat
Smooth, weather-resisting, and double coated. The top coat is close, straight, hard and lies flat. The undercoat is woolly in texture, thick and close, giving the animal good resistance to the cold.

### Colour
With this breed, colour is in itself not important and has no effect on the character of the dog or its fitness to work. However, all-white or near-white is not desired.

### Grooming
A good brush or rub over with the hound glove and a good comb keeps the loose hairs under control and the coat looking good.

### Exercise
This dog needs sensible and regular exercise to keep it in good shape and hard condition.

### Temperament
It is somewhat aloof as well as being intelligent, confident, vigilant and fearless. It is important to select a sturdy-looking puppy with a good, stable temperament.

### Suitability as a family companion
This is an active breed, best for a discerning owner and family. In the right hands, it is a wonderful dog.

This dog originated as a protector of flocks and has become tremendously popular all over the world. It is agile and strong, smooth and well proportioned.

The body should be well boned, with plenty of muscle. The head is long, lean and clean-cut with a slight stop. The muzzle is strong. The eyes are almond-shaped and dark, matching the surrounding coat. They should look straight ahead and have a lively, intelligent expression. The ears are of moderate size, erect and placed rather high on the skull.

There should be good depth of brisket, but the chest should not be too broad. The well feathered tail should reach at least to the hock and never be carried above the back-line. The movement should seem effortless: smooth, rhythmic and long-reaching.

This is a fine, versatile dog that needs to be well understood. If it is treated sensibly it makes a first-rate dog for whatever job it is called upon to do.

# GERMAN SHORTHAIRED POINTER

*Gundog group*

**Size**
Males: 58–64 cm (23–25 ins) 25–31.8 kg (55–70 lbs)
Females: 53–59 cm (21–23 ins) 20.4–27.2 kg (45–60 lbs)

**Coat**
Short, flat and coarse to the touch.

**Colour**
Solid liver, liver-and-white spotted, liver-and-white ticked, liver-and-white spotted and ticked, black-and-white.

**Grooming**
The short coat is easy to manage. It needs a good regular brush.

**Exercise**
An active breed, it will need plenty of exercise. It especially enjoys being able to run free.

**Temperament**
This dog is exceedingly kind and mild, but quite capable of looking after itself if needs be.

**Suitability as a family companion**
With its short coat and clean lines, this increasingly popular gundog is also a good family dog. Ideally, it is more suited to living in the country where there is plenty of space, rather than in the town.

As its name implies, this Pointer comes from Germany. It was based on an old Spanish Pointer as well as Bloodhound and Foxhound. Today's breed is an intelligent, keen and loyal gundog with a good nose, speed and endurance and the look of a thoroughbred.

The head is clean-cut and in balance with the body. The nose is brown, with wide nostrils. The eyes are medium-sized, soft and intelligent and should be of a colour that matches the body.

The ears are broad, set on high and should hang close to the head. The chest should look deep rather than wide, with the ribs well sprung and the back short and firm. The hindquarters are strong and compact, and the feet well padded. The tail should be docked and never be held either bent or high over the back. The movement is smooth and lithe.

The German Shorthair is a medium-sized hunting dog, a true worker and a pleasing family pet.

# GERMAN WIREHAIRED POINTER

*Gundog group*

**Size**
Males: ideally 60–65 cm (23.5–25.5 ins)
25–32 kg (55–70.5 lbs)
Females: no less than 56 cm (22 ins)
20.5–27 kg (45–59.5 lbs)

**Coat**
Very harsh, of medium length, and
close-fitting. It should be abundant,
with a tight undercoat. The coat needs
to be long enough to give good
protection, but should not hide the
body shape.

**Colour**
Solid liver, liver-and-white spotted or
ticked, liver-and-white spotted and
ticked or black-and-white.

**Grooming**
The harsh coat needs a regular brush
and comb, but is easy to manage.

**Exercise**
Understandably, this active gundog
needs plenty of exercise and the
opportunity of a good free run.

**Temperament**
Lively, very obedient and easy to train.
Although it is aloof with strangers, it is
not unfriendly.

**Suitability as a family companion**
This breed is ideally suited to a country
life. It is an adaptable hunter and has
strong guarding instincts. It enjoys
human contact and is an affectionate
dog to have about the home.

**Special needs**
It respects firmness but this should be
tempered with kindness for best results.

This breed evolved in Germany. It is
similar in make-up to the German
Shorthair and is a splendid general
gundog.

The skull is broad and the
bewhiskered muzzle fairly long. The
eyebrows are bushy and the nose is dark
brown with open nostrils. The eyes are
dark hazel, bright and intelligent.

The chest is deep and ribs well
sprung. The back is firm and the
hindquarters strong. The feet should be
round, well padded and tight.

The tail is customarily docked. It
should never be carried high over the
back or be bent. The movement should
be smooth and cover plenty of ground
with each stride.

This is an energetic dog that enjoys
an active life. It needs a home and
background where the family is able to
give some time to its needs. The reward
will be a keen worker and a devoted
companion.

# GIANT SCHNAUZER

*Working group*

**Size**
Males: 70 cm (27.5 ins)
Females: slightly smaller

**Coat**
The outer coat is harsh and wiry, more so on the legs. The undercoat is dense and soft. The beard and eyebrows are prominent.

**Colour**
Either solid black, or the unique pepper-and-salt, which fades into a light grey or silver white on the eyebrows, cheeks, the beard under the throat, on the chest, the legs and under the tail. The pepper-and-salt colouring is shades of grey interspersed with darker guard hairs. The colour can vary from a light silver-grey through to dark steel, depending on the depth and colouring of the banding.

**Grooming**
Regular removal of the full soft undercoat helps keep the coat manageable.

**Exercise**
It does not need a tremendous amount of exercise, but it will always enjoy as much as it is given.

**Temperament**
Intelligent, affectionate and adaptable.

**Suitability as a family companion**
An excellent watchdog, the Giant is companionable and splendid with its family. It has a good life-span, but does take time to grow up.

**Special needs**
This dog needs firm handling, especially in early life, as it can be boisterous and wilful.

The formidable Giant is a splendid, well proportioned and intelligent dog. It was bred as a larger follow-on from the Standard Schnauzer, which originated in Bavaria centuries ago.

The Giant is nearly square: it should give an overall picture of balance and sturdiness, without being either coarse or racy. The head is the distinguishing feature and should be strong and elongated, with a powerful muzzle, enhanced by a prominent beard and eyebrows. The eyes are dark and show plenty of character. They should not be deep set. The ears are neat and 'V'-shaped.

The body is roomy and the chest deep. The back is firm and the tail, customarily docked, is carried erect. Movement should be free-flowing.

With all Schnauzer breeds, emphasis has always been on a functional, utilitarian dog with character rather than on a beautiful one.

# GORDON SETTER

*Gundog group*

**Size**
Males: 66 cm (26 ins) 29.5 kg (65 lbs)
Females: 62 cm (24.5 ins) 25.4 kg (56 lbs)

**Coat**
Silky, flat and of moderate length, with feathering on the legs, breeches, belly, chest and tail.

**Colour**
Deep shining coal-black, with tan markings of rich chestnut-red.

**Grooming**
The coat requires regular brushing and combing.

**Exercise**
This dog is perhaps better suited to the country. It enjoys and needs regular and sufficient exercise. It likes the water.

**Temperament**
It is strong-willed, but easily trained: affectionate and intelligent.

**Suitability as a family companion**
This is a good-tempered and marvellous housedog. Although it is a big animal, it does not take up a lot of houseroom.

**Special needs**
It really should have a good gallop at times.

Of Scottish origins, and the heaviest of the Setters, the Gordon is a stylish dog built on galloping lines. Its striking colour contrast and glossy coat, along with its thoroughbred appearance, makes a most handsome dog.

The head should be fairly long and deep rather than broad but it should still have plenty of brain room. The ears are set on low, lying close to the head and feathered. The eyes should be dark brown and bright, giving a keen intelligent expression. The Gordon has a good deep body with well sprung ribs and plenty of heart and lung room. The tail is short and feathered and the feet should have plenty of hair between the toes.

The handsome Gordon settles well to its surroundings and enjoys life and human company.

# GREAT DANE

*Working group*

**Size**
Males: a minimum of 76 cm (30 ins)
54.5 kg (120 lbs)
Females: a minimum of 71 cm (28 ins)
45.4 kg (100 lbs)

**Coat**
Short, dense and sleek looking. On no account should it incline to roughness.

**Colour**
Brindle, fawn, black, blue, and harlequin. This last is a pure white with irregular black or blue markings.

**Grooming**
The short coat requires the minimum of attention. A good rub with the hound glove will be fine.

**Exercise**
It needs a reasonable amount.

**Temperament**
Good-tempered and highly intelligent.

**Suitability as a family companion**
This dog's nobility and clean lines, combined with a pleasant nature and the fact that it is easily trained has made it popular everywhere. It is good with children.

**Special needs**
Remember, this is a big breed that will need quality feeding at all times, especially when it is growing. It is not the longest-living of breeds. Watch out for damage to the tail, which can sometimes prove a problem in healing.

A giant amongst breeds, the Great Dane was originally used for hunting wild boar. Opinions as to its place of origin are varied: what is certain is that it was not Denmark.

Elegance of outline is essential with this breed, as is an alertness of expression and briskness of movement. The head should be in proportion to the size of the dog. The skull is flat, with a slight indentation running up the centre and a decided rise over the eyes.

The eyes are medium-sized, and preferably dark, and deeply set. Wall or odd eyes are permissible in harlequins.

The body should be very deep. The hindquarters and thighs should be muscular and, the feet should be cat-like with arched toes. The tail is thick at the root and tapers towards the end, reaching at least to the hocks.

# GREYHOUND

*Hound group*

**Size**
Males: 71–76 cm (28–30 ins)
Females: 68–71 cm (27–28 ins)

**Coat**
Fine and close.

**Colour**
Black, white, red, blue, fawn, fallow, brindle or any of these colours broken with white.

**Grooming**
The short coat presents no problems. All it needs is a regular rub down with the hound glove.

**Exercise**
Although the breed possess great stamina and endurance, this does not mean it needs hours of exercise. A good walk on the lead and short free gallop in the park or field will be fine.

**Temperament**
Amiable, intelligent and affectionate.

**Suitability as a family companion**
Greyhounds fit in well with home life. Despite their size, they do not take up a lot of room and they make affectionate and undemanding companions. Owners must accept the need for sensible exercise to keep them in good shape.

**Special needs**
This dog has a tendency to chase anything that runs, so exercise must be carefully supervised.

The Greyhound is a masterpiece, created by the skill of English breeders. It combines a haughty, aristocratic appearance with exceptional skill and speed. It can chase real hares in the open countryside as well as mechanical ones on the race track.

The Greyhound is a strongly built, upstanding dog. The head is long, moderately wide, with a flat skull, slight stop and powerful jaws. The eyes are bright, intelligent and dark. The ears are small, fine-textured and rose-shaped. The neck is long and muscular.

The Greyhound has a deep, capacious chest, providing plenty of heart and lung room. The back is long and broad, with a powerful, slightly arched loin. The hindquarters show great propelling power.

Sound legs and feet are essential. The tail is long, set and carried rather low, strong at the root and slightly curved.

A clean-limbed, robust dog, the Greyhound can be a delightful companion, especially in a sporting household.

# GRIFFON

*Toy group*

### Size
Males and females: 2.3–5 kg (5–11 lbs),
ideally around 2.7–4.5 kg (6–10 lbs)

### Coat
*Rough*: with harsh, wiry texture and
free from curl, preferably with an
undercoat.
*Smooth*: short and tight, with a harsh
feel.

### Colour
Clear red or black, or black and rich
tan. In the clear red, a darker shade on
the mask and ears is desirable. Ideally,
each hair should be an even red from tip
to root.

### Grooming
This dog should be regularly brushed
and combed. The dead coat needs to be
stripped out.

### Exercise
It is happy with a limited amount of
exercise and this makes it an ideal dog
for town life. It also enjoys a walk and a
free run in the park whenever possible.

### Temperament
Alert, perky and game.

### Suitability as a family companion
A companionable breed, obedient and
intelligent, ideal for young or old, and
any kind of home.

This is a smart little dog, with the
disposition of a terrier. It should be well
balanced and square, lively and alert,
and heavy for its size. The head should
be large and rounded, but not domed.
The nose should always be black, as
short as possible, with large open
nostrils. There should be a deep stop
between the nose and skull.

The chin is prominent and slightly
undershot without showing the teeth,
the muzzle is wide and the roughs have
a good beard. The eyes are very dark,
large and round. They are clear and
alert, all giving a pert, monkey-like
expression. The chest is wide and deep,
with well muscled hindquarters and a
level back. The tail is carried high and is
customarily docked to the required
length. The Griffon should move with
freedom and purpose.

This is a breed with great charm and
character, delightful about the home
whatever size.

# HUNGARIAN PULI

*Working group*

**Size**
Males: 40–44 cm (16–17.5 ins) 13–15 kg (28.5–33 lbs)
Females: 37–41 cm (14–16 ins) 10–13 kg (22–28.5 lbs)

**Coat**
The whole dog is covered with a thick, weather-resisting coat that forms natural narrow cords made from a good top and undercoat. The coat is generally longest on the hindquarters and shortest on the head and feet. Some dogs will grow a coat to floor length.

**Colour**
Acceptable colours are black, rusty-black, apricot and various shades of grey-and-white. The black may sometimes appear weathered and rusty or slightly grey. A very small breast spot is acceptable, as are a few white hairs on the feet. With this breed, the whole skin should be well pigmented and slate-grey.

**Grooming**
The coat looks difficult to groom, but a regular bath and teasing and separating of the cords into shape with your fingers keeps it as it should be. The cording starts to form at around nine months or so. If you get them into shape from the beginning they will hang in even, tight twists and not need all that much attention. A brush and comb is not used on this breed.

**Exercise**
Although this is a herding breed that is active and lively, it is not demanding in its exercise needs.

**Temperament**
Lively, intelligent, undemanding and faithful. It also has a sense of humour.

**Suitability as a family companion**
The Puli makes an excellent, if unusual, housedog. It is a good watch-dog and fine with the children. It is home-loving and affectionate and trains easily.

The Puli is one of several varieties of sheep-dog that have been in Hungary for more than a thousand years.

It should look square, with a small, fine head and a slightly domed skull. The muzzle is blunt and is one third the length of the head. The stop is well defined and the nose is large and black. The dark brown, medium-sized eyes should have a lively expression. The ears are set just below the skull.

The ribs are deep, broad and well sprung. The hindquarters are strong and the feet are round and tight. The tail is of medium length and curled tightly over the rump.

With this breed, the movement is unusual, as the stride is not far-reaching and the gallop is short, in harmony with its lively disposition. It should not be heavy, lethargic or lumbering.

Its alertness, quick response and trainability are great assets in the Puli, while its unique coat and somewhat unkempt appearance make it an unusual dog.

# HUNGARIAN VIZSLA

*Gundog group*

**Size**
Males: ideally, 57–64 cm (22.5–25 ins)
22–30 kg (48.5–66 lbs)
Females: ideally, 53–60 cm (21–23.5 ins)
22–30 kg (48.5–66 lbs)

**Coat**
Short and straight, dense and coarse
with a somewhat greasy feel.

**Colour**
Russet-gold. Any small white markings
on the chest and feet are acceptable, but
not desirable.

**Grooming**
A good brush or rub over with the
hound glove will keep this short coat in
good order.

**Exercise**
It needs, and enjoys, a good free run
and a reasonable amount of exercise.

**Temperament**
Good-natured, affectionate and lively.

**Suitability as a family companion**
The Vizsla is at its best in a sporting,
country home. Its easy-to-manage short
coat and clean lines are fine for the
house and its affectionate nature makes
it a nice dog to own.

Bred for farmwork on the plains of
Hungary, the lightly-built Vizsla is a
breed of great antiquity. It was not
really known outside its homeland until
this century.

It should have a gaunt and noble
head, fairly wide between the ears and
with a moderate stop. The muzzle
should be a little longer than the skull,
the jaw strong and the nose brown, with
well developed nostrils. The eyes should
be oval and brown: a shade darker than
the coat. The ears are fairly low-set and
hang down close to the cheeks. The
chest is moderately broad and deep,
with a prominent breast-bone.

The hindquarters are well developed.
The feet are round and tight and the tail
is rather low set, and customarily
docked to the required length. It should
be carried horizontally when the dog is
moving. The movement should be
graceful and elegant.

# IBIZAN HOUND

*Hound group*

**Size**
Males and females: 56–74 cm (22–29 ins). This is a large size variance, but overall balance is important.

**Coat**
Either smooth or rough, always hard and close, longer on the tail and the back of the legs.

**Colour**
White, chestnut or fawn, or any combination of these.

**Grooming**
With its easy-to-manage coat, a regular brush and attention to its ears and nails is all this dog needs.

**Exercise**
Being a Greyhound type, it needs plenty of exercise.

**Temperament**
Kind, active and intelligent.

**Suitability as a family companion**
As long as you can give this dog the exercise it needs, it is fine. It is very good with children and its own family, but it can be somewhat reserved with strangers.

**Special needs**
It is a big hound which takes time to develop and mature. It should be allowed this without overdoing things.

This ancient breed was nurtured on the Spanish island of Ibiza. It will work in groups as well as alone, using scent as much as sight. It finds its own game and will often jump high or stand on its hind legs to see the line the game takes. It will retrieve to hand.

It is tall and narrowly built, with distinctive, erect ears. Its head is fine and long, with a flat skull and slight stop. The jaw is lean and the nose flesh-coloured. The expressive eyes are amber and almond-shaped.

The back is level and the rib-cage long and flat. The breastbone is prominent, the hindquarters are long and straight, which helps with the breed's great manouverability.

The tail is long, set low and should reach well below the hock. It may be carried high when excited. This dog moves with a far-reaching stride, hovering slightly before placing its foot on the ground.

# IRISH SETTER

*Gundog group*

**Size**
Males and females: approximately 55 cm (25 ins)

**Coat**
Silky, of moderate length and flat, as free as possible from curl and wave. There should be feathering on legs, breeches and tail, and a good belly fringe which may extend on chest and throat.

**Colour**
Rich chestnut-red.

**Grooming**
It is easy to care for with a good regular brush, and the occasional bath.

**Exercise**
A racy breed that needs regular and sufficient free exercise.

**Temperament**
Energetic, intelligent and affectionate.

**Suitability as a family companion**
Good-tempered and kindly: especially good with children.

**Special needs**
This dog matures slowly, so you will have to deal with puppy traits and high spirits for some time. The adult needs a lot of regular exercise and must be allowed to run freely.

This is a gundog, built on racier lines than the other Setters. The head is long and lean with a moderately deep muzzle, fairly square at the end. The nose should be dark mahogany walnut, or black.

The ears are of moderate length and of fine texture, set low and hanging in a neat fold, close to the skull. The eyes should have a kindly expression. They are dark hazel or dark brown.

The neck should be moderately long and muscular, but not too thick. The chest is deep and the hindquarters are wide and powerful. The tail is set on low, strong at the root and tapering to a fine point.

The Irish Setter is well suited to country life but will settle well in town as long as it has the opportunity for free exercise in the park.

# IRISH TERRIER

*Terrier group*

**Size**
Males: 46 cm (18 ins) 12.2 kg (27 lbs)
Females: 46 cm (18 ins) 11.3 kg (25 lbs)

**Coat**
Hard, wiry, straight and flat, with a broken appearance, and a finer, softer undercoat. The topcoat should be free from any silkiness or softness.

**Colour**
Bright red, red-wheaten or yellow-wheaten. A small white spot on the chest is frequently seen in self-coloured breeds.

**Grooming**
This is another rough-coated terrier breed whose coat needs to be stripped regularly. It should be combed through several times a week to prevent any tangling and matts in the furnishings.

**Exercise**
This dog enjoys what exercise you can give it, but it is quite content with its home and garden.

**Temperament**
This is the dare-devil of the canine world: it has the heart of a lion, but is remarkably good-tempered and happy with children.

**Suitability as a family companion**
This is a hardy, game terrier which needs sensible and firm handling as a puppy. It will repay this with extraordinary devotion.

**Special needs**
The Irish Terrier can be firey with other dogs, especially when provoked but, if this is taken into account, it should not give any trouble.

This dog originated in Ireland. It should give the immediate impression of an active, lively, lithe and wiry dog with plenty of substance.

The head should be long, with a flat skull and should be rather narrow between the ears. There is a little goatee beard and eyebrows. The jaw should be strong and muscular. The eyes are small and dark, full of intelligence, life and fire. The ears are set well on the head, and should be small, 'V'-shaped, and of moderate thickness.

A deep and muscular body of moderate length is desired, and the hindquarters should be powerful, strong and muscular. The feet should be strong, round and moderately small, with arched toes. The tail is customarily docked, and should be set on high and carried erect.

Anyone looking for a good-sized terrier, not quite as big as the Airedale, could well choose the Irish.

# IRISH WOLFHOUND

*Hound group*

**Size**
Males: 79 cm (31 ins) minimum.
Breeders aim for 81–86 cm (32–34 ins)
Females: 71 cm (28 ins) minimum.
Breeders aim for 73 cm (31 ins)

**Coat**
Rough and hardy with good undercoat.
The hair is somewhat longer over the
eyes and under the jaw.

**Colour**
All shades of brindle, with grey
predominating. It can be red, cream,
wheaten and black.

**Grooming**
Regular grooming is important,
especially when the coat sheds and the
undercoat comes out.

**Exercise**
It needs a good daily gallop.

**Temperament**
Friendly, gentle and trusting.

**Suitability as a family companion**
This dog is not really suitable for town
life, but it can adapt to any
surroundings. It is intelligent and
reflective rather than lively, and is the
most good-natured and delightful of
companions.

**Special needs**
With a quick-growing breed like this,
wise feeding and rearing are essential.
Do not overburden the growing dog
with too much exercise and do not let it
get too fat. The tail can be a problem if
it is damaged, as it is slow to heal.

The Irish Wolfhound is rugged and
muscular, yet graceful and commanding
in appearance. It is the national dog of
Ireland and the tallest of all dogs.

The head and muzzle are long, with
little indentation between the eyes. The
skull is not too broad. The eyes are dark
and the ears small.

The neck is long and muscular, well
arched and without any loose skin
about the throat. The front legs should
be strong and quite straight and the
chest has good breadth and depth. The
hindquarters are strong and muscular.
The feet are fairly large and round. The
tail is long, moderately thick, covered
with hair and slightly curved.

Despite its imposing appearance and
size, the Irish Wolfhound has an even
temperament, is loyal and affectionate
to its owner and makes a noble,
charming and good-natured companion.

# ITALIAN GREYHOUND

*Toy group*

### Size
Males and females: ideally 2.7–3.6 kg
(6–8 lbs). No more than 4.5 kg (10 lbs)

### Coat
Thin and glossy, like satin. The skin
should be fine and supple.

### Colour
All shades of fawn, white, cream, blue,
black-and-fawn, and white pied.

### Grooming
A brush or rub down with a chamois
leather is all that is needed.

### Exercise
The freedom of the garden will be quite
enough for this dog, but it enjoys walks
and a run in the park.

### Temperament
This dog is lively, intelligent, loyal and
faithful.

### Suitability as a family companion
This affectionate toy breed makes an
excellent family dog. It is well built and
robust, despite its delicate appearance.

This is an elegant and graceful breed
which enjoyed great popularity among
the aristocracy of the 17th and 18th
centuries. Its characteristic movement is
easy and graceful. Its soft coat, the lines
of its body, its lively intelligence and
unsurpassed fidelity makes a truly
distinctive small dog.

The head should be long, flat and
narrow, with a very fine muzzle. The
eyes should be rather large, bright and
full of expression. The ears are soft and
delicate and placed well back. The neck
is gracefully arched and the body has a
deep, narrow chest, with a slight curve
to the back. The bone is fine and the
hindquarters muscular. The tail is rather
long, fine and set on low.

This is an aristocratic little breed,
which is both bright and charming. It is
quite undemanding in its needs and
makes a good family pet.

# JAPANESE CHIN

*Toy group*

**Size**
Males and females: 1.8–3.2 kg (4–7 lbs)

**Coat**
Profuse, long, soft and straight of silky texture. It should be free of curl or wave and have a tendency to stand out, especially at the frill of the neck.

**Colour**
Black-and-white or red-and-white. Red includes all shades: sable, brindle, lemon and orange. The brighter and clearer the red the better. The colour should be evenly distributed on the cheeks and ears and as patches on the body. It should not be too heavily marked. The white should be clear and not flecked.

**Grooming**
A daily brush and comb and an occasional bath will keep this dog in good form. Do not forget a regular check to see that the ears are clean and the nails short.

**Exercise**
The freedom of a garden, even a small one, will give this dog all the exercise it needs.

**Suitability as a family companion**
It is an ideal dog for both town and country.

The Japanese Chin is a smart, dainty little dog, especially stylish in movement. The head is large, but in proportion to the size of the dog. The muzzle is very short and wide and well-cushioned, the nostrils are big and the eyes large, dark and set wide apart. The white should show in the inner corners: this gives the all-important look of astonishment that is so typical and valued in the breed. The ears are well feathered.

The body should be cobby in shape, and wide in chest. The hindquarters have profuse feathering on the thighs. The tail is also profusely feathered, and carried over the back.

A good-tempered little dog with a lot of personality, the Japanese Chin is an excellent pet.

# JAPANESE SPITZ

*Utility group*

**Size**
Males: 30–40 cm (12–16 ins)
Females: 25–35 cm (10–14 ins)

**Coat**
The outer, long coat should be straight and stand-off, with a mane on the neck and shoulder, and profuse long hair on the tail. The undercoat is soft in texture, dense, short and profuse.

**Colour**
Pure white.

**Grooming**
Do not be put off by the pure white coat. This is a fastidious dog that does not like getting dirty. A good comb and occasional bath, or a clean with a quality coat dressing and then a blow dry, keeps it in sparkling order.

**Exercise**
It is happy within its own home and garden but, like all dogs, it enjoys a run in the park.

**Temperament**
It is affectionate, happy, lively and obedient.

**Suitability as a family companion**
This dog is devoted to its family and is a good mixer. It is an ideal family dog whose sharp hearing makes it a good watchdog.

This small Spitz breed is a recent development in Japan, but its exact history is difficult to trace.

It has a wedge-shaped head, moderately broad and slightly rounded. The stop is well defined, and the muzzle sharply pointed. The nose is small and black. The eyes should be almond-shaped, moderately sized, not too far apart and dark, with black eye rims. The ears are erect, small and triangular, set high and not too wide apart.

The chest should be broad and deep and the hindlegs moderately angulated. The nails should be black or dark and the feet round and cat-like. Its movement is smooth and nimble. The tail is of moderate length, set high and curled over the back.

This is a delightful and appealing dog, especially when it is a puppy. It has a good life expectancy and will prove an amusing, intelligent and affectionate companion.

# KEESHOUND

*Utility group*

**Size**
Males: 45.7 cm (18 ins)
Females: 43 cm (17 ins)

**Coat**
Dense, harsh, and off-standing. It should have a dense ruff and well-feathered, profuse trousers. Soft, thick, light-coloured undercoat. The coat should not be silky, wavy or woolly, nor should it form a parting on the back.

**Colour**
Should be a wolf-like ash-grey not all black or all white.

**Grooming**
It needs a regular, good, deep, down-to-the-skin brush and comb, especially when the coat is shedding.

**Exercise**
It will take as much or as little exercise as you care to give, and it will be content with that.

**Temperament**
This is a real extrovert: friendly to both people and other dogs. It is neither timid nor belligerent.

**Suitability as a family companion**
Its excellent disposition and patience make it a splendid companion, especially with children.

**Special needs**
It is important the puppy gets used to regular grooming and learns from an early age not to be noisy.

Known as the Dutch Barge Dog. The Keeshound was used as a guard dog, especially on the barges of the Netherlands and of Germany. Its small frame and acute hearing made it ideal.

The head should be wedge-shaped, with a definite stop. The muzzle is of medium length. The eyes are dark brown and almond-shaped and have a gentle expression. There should be light grey hair around the eyes which are outlined by distinctive dark 'spectacles'.

The small, pointed ears are neat and well set on the head. The nose, eye rims and lips are jet black, giving a rather foxy look. The breed has a short compact body and alert carriage. The well feathered, curling tail is carried over the back.

The Keeshound is an adaptable and easy-to-keep breed, as long as one pays attention to regular grooming, and does not overfeed the adult if it leads a sedentary life. It is a delightful character.

# KERRY BLUE TERRIER

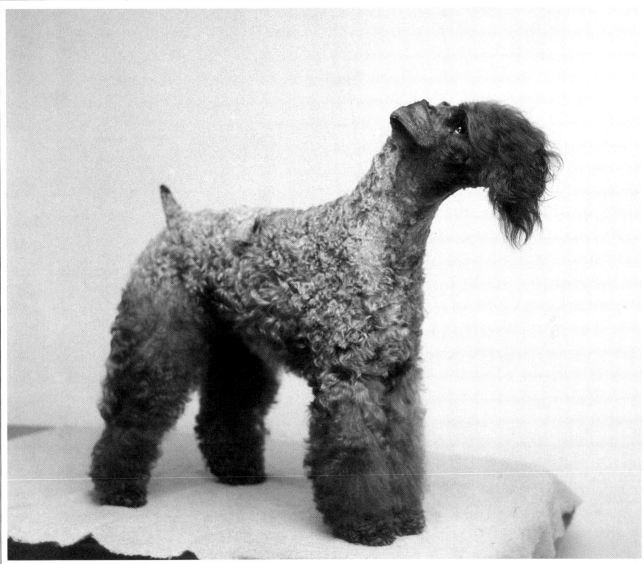

*Terrier group*

**Size**
Males: 46–48 cm (18–19 ins) 16 kg (35 lbs)
Females: slightly less

**Coat**
Soft, silky, plentiful and wavy.

**Colour**
The Kerry is born black and will not start to get its true colouring (any shade of blue, with or without black points) until it is about 18 months old. A small white spot on the chest is acceptable.

**Grooming**
The Kerry's coat needs regular attention. Its shape is created by scissor work. A daily combing stops matts and tangles forming.

**Exercise**
An active dog, the Kerry needs a daily walk.

**Temperament**
It is a game but disciplined dog and will not fight unless provoked.

**Suitability as a family companion**
Good with children and a splendid guard, the Kerry is a one-person dog and a good companion.

The Kerry Blue originated in the mountains of Kerry in the south-west of Ireland. It was first bred and used to hunt badgers and foxes, but has also proved to be a good guard for livestock.

The Kerry's head should be well balanced, long and lean. It should have a flat skull and a slight stop. The foreface and jaws are very strong. The eyes are small to medium-sized, as dark as possible, giving a keen terrier expression. The ears are small, 'V'-shaped and are not carried as high as in some terrier breeds.

It should have a well developed and muscular body. The back should be straight and the hindquarters powerful. The tail is customarily docked and is set on high and carried erect. The feet should be round and small, and the toenails should be black.

Although the Kerry has a coat that needs a reasonable amount of attention, this should not deter those seeking a medium-sized, adaptable and game terrier.

# LAKELAND TERRIER

*Terrier group*

**Size**
Males: no more than 36.8 cm (14.5 ins)
7.7 kg (171 lbs)
Females: no more than 36.8 cm (14.5 ins) 6.8 kg (15 lbs)

**Coat**
Dense and weather-resisting, it has a harsh texture. There should be a good undercoat.

**Colour**
Black-and-tan, blue-and-tan, red, wheaten, red-grizzle, liver, blue or black. Small tips of white on the feet and chest will not debar it in the show ring. Mahogany or deep tan is not typical.

**Grooming**
The Lakeland is one of the terrier breeds which need trimming, usually twice a year. A regular brush and comb to the furnishings and body coat keeps tangles at bay. This dog does not shed its coat.

**Exercise**
It is happy within the garden, but enjoys walks and free runs.

**Temperament**
Gay and fearless.

**Suitability as a family companion**
This handy-sized terrier is a most suitable family dog. It is alert as a guard, has a good bark and sharp hearing, and can be an ideal companion.

**Special needs**
One must accept the coat will need regular attention, otherwise the breed makes few demands and is most adaptable.

As one would expect from its name, this smart and workman-like terrier originated in the Lake District. In its early days it was known as the Westmorland or Cumberland Terrier. The head should be well balanced, with a flat and refined skull, the muzzle powerful and the nose black. The eyes are dark or hazel. The ears are moderately small, 'V'-shaped, and should be carried alertly.

The breed should have good bone, the chest is reasonably narrow, and the back should be strong and moderately short. The hindquarters are strong and powerful. The feet should be small, compact, round and well padded. The tail, which is customarily docked, is set high and carried gaily, but it should not curl over the back.

If you are looking for a companionable, handy-sized and adaptable terrier, the Lakeland is one to think about.

# LARGE MUNSTLANDER

*Gundog group*

**Size**
Males: 61 cm (24 ins) 25–29.5 kg (55–65 lbs) (approximately)
Females: 58 cm (23 ins) 25 kg (55 lbs) (approximately)

**Coat**
Long and dense, but not curly or coarse. Good feathering on the legs and tail, with short and smooth-lying hair on the head.

**Colour**
The head is solid black with a white blaze, snip (small patches) or star allowed. The body colour is white with black patches, or blue roan with black patches, flecked, ticked, or a combination of these.

**Grooming**
It has straightforward requirements: just a good brush and comb a couple of times a week.

**Exercise**
Being an active, muscular dog, exercise is most important for this breed if it is to be kept in good, hard, healthy condition.

**Temperament**
The Munstlander is loyal, affectionate and trustworthy.

**Suitability as a family companion**
Although this is not yet a well known breed, it is fine in a sporting home.

This gundog originated in Germany, where it is extremely popular with sportsmen. Elsewhere, it is gaining many friends, who appreciate its trainability, good nose, staying power and the fact that it is a good worker both on land and in the water.

The skull should be broad, with strong jaw muscles. The nose should be black with wide nostrils and the eyes should be dark brown. The ears are feathered and set high.

The body is firm and muscular and the back strong. The ribs should be deep and well sprung. The chest is wide and the hindquarters are well muscled. The feet should be tight and well padded, with hair between the toes. The movement should show plenty of drive.

The last one or two joints of the tail are often docked, for practical reasons. They are easily damaged as the dog thrashes its tail, and amputation is often necessary.

# LHASA APSO

*Utility group*

**Size**
Males: 25.5 cm (10 ins)
Females: slightly less

**Coat**
Heavy straight hard topcoat of good length, not woolly or silky. The undercoat is dense.

**Colour**
All shades of golden, dark grizzle, slate, smoke, black, white, brown or parti-coloured.

**Grooming**
The coat is the breeds' crowning glory and repays all the care and attention given to it. An occasional bath and a regular brush and comb is essential. The hair on the head can be caught up in a grip to keep it out of the eyes. It is a good idea to keep the coat ends scissored at leg length during the winter.

**Exercise**
The Lhasa enjoys plenty of exercise in all forms, but will not demand it.

**Temperament**
Affectionate, loyal, gay and assertive.

**Suitability as a family companion**
A small breed of great charm and character, the Lhasa is a splendid companion. It is intelligent, affectionate and adaptable in town or country. It loves human company.

**Special needs**
Keep the ears clean and the nails short, and make sure the hair between the pads is cut short.

This well balanced, solid little dog has a moderately narrow skull. The foreface is straight, with a medium stop and a dark nose. The eyes are also dark. The head is heavily furnished, with good whiskers and a beard and a frill over the eyes. The ears should be well feathered and the neck has a mane, more pronounced in dogs than bitches.

The body is compact. The front legs are straight and the hindquarters well developed. Both back and front legs are well covered with hair. The feet should be cat-like, with good pads.

Ideally, this breed should be well feathered between the pads, but it is best to cut this hair short so that the dog does not end up walking on a bed of hair. The tail is feathered, set high and carried over the back. There is often a kink at the end.

This bright, hardy little dog is in no way a toy or lap dog. It was bred for centuries in the villages of Tibet, essentially as a watch-dog.

# LOWCHEN

*Toy group*

**Size**
Males and females: ideally 25–32.5 cm (10–13 ins)

**Coat**
Fairly long and wavy, but not curly. Thick and silky.

**Colour**
Any whole or parti-colour or mixture of colours is permissible.

**Grooming**
The breed has a particular trim with the hindquarters. Part of the body and tail and front legs are clipped short, leaving a profuse mane effect with pom-poms on the ankles and end of the tail. All this gives a lion-like effect, and the breed is sometimes called 'the little lion-dog'. The coat is easy to brush and comb.

**Exercise**
This dog is generally active and enjoys a good walk, but it is quite happy to exercise within the garden.

**Temperament**
A lovely temperament, affectionate and friendly.

**Suitability as a family companion**
An easy-to-manage breed with lots of charm. It is hardy, does not moult and is quite delightful as a family pet.

This fascinating and intelligent little dog dates back to the 13th century. It originated in the Mediterranean countries where it was popular with the Florentine noblemen and court ladies. The clip originated in those times when it was used as a living hot-water-bottle!

The head should be carried high and should have a fairly broad skull which should be flat between the ears. The stop is well defined and the muzzle short and strong. The nose should be black, eyes should be dark, round and large giving an intelligent, sweet expression. The ears are long and well fringed. The body is well proportioned with a short back, hindquarters have a good turn of stifle. The feet are small and round. The tail is carried gaily with the plume falling over the dog's back.

The Lowchen is gaining many friends, for it combines all the good qualities of a companion dog.

# MALTESE

*Toy group*

**Size**
Males and females: no more than 25.5
cm (10 ins)

**Coat**
The coat has a silky texture, straight
and of good length.

**Colour**
Pure white, though slight lemon
markings are not considered wrong.

**Grooming**
This breed looks much better if it is
regularly combed, and bathed when it is
grubby.

**Exercise**
The Maltese will get enough exercise in
the garden, or on a walk around the
block. But in enjoys a longer walk, or a
romp in the park.

**Temperament**
It is a sweet-tempered, vivacious and
very intelligent dog.

**Suitability as a family companion**
Lively and alert, the Maltese is
extremely good with children and is
ideal as a family pet. It fits in especially
well in a town house or flat.

**Special needs**
Grooming is essential, as the coat is one
of the dog's main attractions. Wipe the
eyes daily, as these dogs are prone to
tear-stain.

This type of dog is of very ancient
origin and is thought by some
authorities to have been known and
highly prized in Roman times.

It is an alert little dog, whose body
should look short, cobby and well
balanced. It should have a good spring
of rib and level back. The head should
be balanced, with a well defined stop.
The nose and eye-rims should be pure
black and the eyes dark brown. The ears
are long and well feathered, the hair
mingling with the coat at the shoulder.
The legs are short and straight and the
hindquarters nicely angulated. The legs
are short and straight and the
hindquarters nicely angulated. Pigment
is important: the pads and nails should
be black. The tail is arched over the
back and covered with abundant hair.
The movement should be free.

This smart and elegant breed repays
all the care and attention it needs by
being a lively and devoted companion.

# MANCHESTER TERRIER

*Terrier group*

**Size**
Males: 40.5 cm (16 ins)
Females: 38 cm (15 ins)

**Coat**
Close, smooth, short and glossy. It
should be weatherproof.

**Colour**
Jet black and rich mahogany tan. On
the head, the muzzle should be tanned
to the nose, and the nasal bone should
be black. There should be a small tan
spot on each cheek and above each eye.
The underjaw and the throat should be
tanned with a distinct 'V'. The legs are
tanned from the knees down to the toes,
which should be pencilled with black.
There is a distinctive black 'thumb
mark' immediately above the feet. The
inside of the hindlegs should be tanned,
with black at the stifle joint. The area

under the tail should be tanned and
there should be a slight tan mark on
each side of the chest. In all cases, the
division between the colours should be
clearly defined. Tan outside the hind
legs, called 'breeching', is a defect.

**Grooming**
The short coat presents no problems. A
good brush and rub with a cloth will be
fine.

**Exercise**
This dog is happy with a good walk,
and freedom of the garden.

**Temperament**
Alert, boisterous and quick to learn.

**Suitability as a family companion**
Fiercely loyal to its owners and family
and a good house dog, it proves a
splendid family pet. It is good with
children.

Over the last hundred years,
Manchesters have been divided into two
separate groups. The larger became
known as the Manchester Terrier, and
the smaller developed into the English
Toy Terrier (Black-and-tan).

With its clean lines, handy size and
good temperament, this breed deserves
to be more popular than it is. Overall,
this should be a compact dog, with
good bone. The head is long and wedge-
shaped, with a flat skull. The eyes
should be dark, oblong, small and
sparkling. The ears are 'V'-shaped, neat,
small and carried well above the topline
of the skull.

The breed has a narrow, deep chest
and should be well sprung. The feet
should be strong and semi-hare-footed,
with well arched toes. The tail is short,
tapering to a point and should not be
carried higher than the level of the back.

# MAREMMA

*Working group*

**Size**
Males: at least 65 cm (25.5 ins)
Females: at least 59.5 (23.5 ins)

**Coat**
The coat should be long, plentiful and rather harsh. It can be slightly wavy but no curliness is permitted. The hair forms a thick collar on the neck and is short on the muzzle, the head, ears, feet and front of limbs but should form a slight feathering on the rear edges of the limbs. The undercoat is thick and close.

**Colour**
White, ivory or pale fawn, with or without slightly darker shadings.

**Grooming**
The good dense, weather resisting coat needs a regular and good brush with a bristle brush, and then a comb through. Pay special attention to behind the ears, thighs and tail, especially when the coat is shedding.

**Exercise**
Being an active sheepdog, exercise is important, and it should be adequate to keep it in good shape and condition.

**Temperament**
This is a loyal, intelligent and lively dog.

**Suitability as a family companion**
This is a large breed, best for anyone looking for a majestic and impressive family dog that will prove a good guard.

The Maremma originated in central Italy as a sheepdog. It is a large, strongly-built and sturdy dog.

The head is large, with a skull that is rather wide between the ears and narrow towards the facial area. The muzzle should be slightly shorter than the skull and the jaws are powerful. The nose and lips should be black, the eyes brown, bold and almond-shaped. The ears are small and 'V'-shaped and set high. When in repose, they hang flat but the dog lifts them when it is alert.

The hindquarters are wide and powerful. The feet are oval with close, well arched toes. The tail is set on low and carried low in repose, curling into the horizontal at hock level. It may be carried above the level of the hock when the dog is excited.

# MASTIFF

*Working group*

**Size**
No size is given in the standard, but good minimum heights are:
Males: 75 cm (30 ins)
Females: 70 cm (28 ins)

**Coat**
Short and close-lying, but not too fine over the shoulders, neck and back. The undercoat should be dense and close-lying.

**Colour**
Apricot or silver-fawn, or dark fawn-brindle. The muzzle, ears and nose should be black.

**Grooming**
All it needs is a regular good brush.

**Exercise**
This dog prefers exercising at its own pace.

**Temperament**
Quiet and good-natured. Look for a friendly, outgoing puppy.

**Suitability as a family companion**
Its size and strength may be a disadvantage in a small home. If you do have room, its character and equable temperament make it an excellent companion and guard.

This ancient British breed had been a friend and protector of people and their property for centuries.

The Mastiff should combine a large and well built frame with good nature, courage and docility. The head should look massive, and muscles in the cheeks should be extremely powerful.

There should be marked wrinkling on the dog's face when it is attentive. The muzzle is short and broad under the eyes, ending blunt and square-cut. The stop is well marked and the hazel-brown eyes small and wide apart.

The chest is wide and deep and the back, loins and hindquarters are all broad and muscular. The feet are large.

As long as you have the room, the loyal and faithful Mastiff makes an ideal companion and guard.

# MINIATURE PINSCHER

*Toy group*

**Size**
Males and females: 25.5–30.5 cm (10–12 ins)

**Coat**
Smooth, hard and close fitting. It should be straight and lustrous.

**Colour**
Black, blue and chocolate, with sharply defined tan markings on cheeks, lips, lower jaw, twin spots above eye and on the chest, lower half of the forelegs, the inside of hindlegs and vent region, and the lower portion of hocks and feet. These colours should have black pencilling on the toes. The breed can also be solid red of various shades.

**Grooming**
With this short coat, a brush and rub over with a soft cloth is sufficient.

**Exercise**
This dog will take exercise and enjoy it, but it will be quite content exercising within the garden.

**Temperament**
Lively and intelligent.

**Suitability as a family companion**
Its size and smooth coat along with its character makes it a good family pet. It is sharp with hearing and gives good warning.

**Special needs**
Do not pamper this dog, but like any small, short coated breed, it needs sensible care, especially when it is extremely hot, cold or wet.

The 'Min Pin', as it is sometimes called, is a sturdy, compact and elegant dog of German origin.

The head is fairly long, and free from any cheekiness, and the muzzle should be strong. The eyes should be black or nearly black, and should fit well into the face, being neither too full nor too round.

The ears are either erect or drop, and should be set on high. The chest is moderately broad and well developed, while the back is sturdy and square. The back slopes slightly towards the rear, and the hindquarters are well developed. The tail, which is customarily docked, is carried high. The feet should be cat-like.

This is a proud and fearless toy breed that makes a smart and attractive companion.

# NEWFOUNDLAND

*Working group*

**Size**
Males: 71 cm (28 ins) 63.6–68 kg (140–150 lbs)
Females: 66 cm (26 ins) 50–54.5 kg (110–120 lbs)

**Coat**
The dog is double coated. The topcoat is flat and dense, of a coarse texture and oily nature. It is capable of resisting water. If it is brushed the wrong way it should fall back into its place naturally. The undercoat is soft and dense.

**Colour**
Black, brown and Landseer. The black should be a dull jet black and the brown should be chocolate or bronze. A splash of white on the chest and toes is acceptable in both colours as is a slight tinge of bronze with the blacks. The Landseer is white, with black markings. These should be a black head with narrow blaze, even-marked saddle and black rump, extending on to the tail.

**Grooming**
The Newfoundland needs an all-over good, regular deep-down comb, paying special attention to behind the ears and the armpits to prevent matts. Give it more frequent combing when it is shedding its coat.

**Exercise**
An adult will require a moderate amount to keep it fit.

**Temperament**
Intelligent, gentle and docile.

**Suitability as a family companion**
The breed has a mild guarding instinct, but is also gentle and has a great affinity with children. It loves human company, delighting in pleasing its owners.

**Special needs**
A Newfoundland puppy needs good quality feeding throughout its growing period. As an adult, it is a heavy dog with big paws, which creates a lot of housework, especially in bad weather.

The breed takes its name from the Canadian island of Newfoundland. Its ancestors are thought to have included the Portuguese Water Dog which, along with only a handful of other breeds (including the Newfoundland), has webbed feet. The Newfoundland loves water.

Its head should be broad with a short, rather square muzzle. The eyes are rather small, dark brown and deeply set.

The back should be broad and the loins strong. The hindquarters are very strong and the thick tail, well covered with hair, reaches the hocks.

Despite its cuddly 'teddy-bear' look as a puppy, it is important to remember that the Newfoundland will grow into a very large dog and will require a lot of attention, regular grooming and an adequate, well balanced diet. However, for anyone seeking a robust, impressive and noble breed with a lovely temperament, the Newfoundland has few rivals.

# NORFOLK TERRIER

*Terrier group*

**Size**
Males and females: ideally 25.4 cm (10 ins)

**Coat**
Hard, wiry and straight, lying close to the body. Longer and rougher on the neck and shoulders. Slight whiskers and eyebrows.

**Colour**
All shades of red, red wheaten, black-and-tan or grizzle.

**Grooming**
A straightforward coat that requires a regular brush and comb, and a trim twice a year.

**Exercise**
It likes walking and will take unlimited exercise, but is also quite at home in a flat or small house, getting only a walk in the park.

**Temperament**
It has a lovable disposition and is not quarrelsome.

**Suitability as a family companion**
This is a loving family dog. Human company is important to it. In return for your care and attention, you will have a delightful companion.

**Special needs**
It hates to be shut away in kennels. It really needs to be with its family.

Originating in East Anglia, this low-to-the-ground terrier is very like its cousin the Norwich Terrier. The skull is wide and slightly rounded, with a shortish muzzle. The eyes are dark brown or black, oval and deep set, giving a keen, alert expression. The ears are 'V'-shaped, dropping forward, close to the cheek. The body should be sturdy, compact and have well sprung ribs. The back should be level and the tail, which is customarily docked, is carried upright. The hindquarters should be well muscled and strong.

This is a small, hardy terrier which is both a delightful, handy-sized companion and a good watchdog.

# NORWEGIAN BUHUND

*Working group*

**Coat**
Close-lying and harsh, with a soft wool undercoat.

**Colour**
Wheaten (biscuit), black, red (so long as the red is not too dark) and wolf-sable. Symmetrical white markings are permitted, although whole colours are preferred. A black mask, ears and black tip to the tail are also permissible.

**Grooming**
A daily brush and combing is needed, especially during the moult.

**Exercise**
It enjoys regular exercise and a free run, but will settle for less.

**Temperament**
This dog has a gay and lively nature, with a touch of independence or stubbornness. It is very loyal.

**Suitability as a family companion**
This is a most suitable family dog: easily trained, good with children and trouble-free.

**Special needs**
It can be noisy, and has a tendency to round anything up. It should be trained not to behave in this way.

The Buhund originated, as its name implies, in Norway. It is a utilitarian farm dog, with plenty of character and energy. *Bu* means the mountain hut where the shepherd lived while tending the herds during the summer.

The Buhund is lightly built. It should have a short, compact body and present a well balanced picture, free from all exaggeration and coarseness. The wedge-shaped head is lean and light. The eyes are dark brown and lively, with a fearless expression. The ears are erect, sharply pointed and very mobile. The tail is set high. It is tightly curled, and may even be double-curled.

In many ways this is an ideal house and family dog: strong, healthy and a convenient size.

# NORWICH TERRIER

*Terrier group*

### Size
Males and females: ideally 25.4 cm (10 ins)
This ideal height should not, however, be attained by excessive length of leg.

### Coat
Hard, wiry and straight, lying close to the body. It has slight whiskers and eyebrows, and a slight ruff to frame the face, framed by longer and rougher hair on the neck.

### Colour
All shades of red, wheaten, grizzle or black-and-tan.

### Grooming
A straightforward easy-to-manage coat that requires trimming twice a year and a regular brush and comb.

### Exercise
This dog is active and will take unlimited exercise, though it is equally happy within its own garden or with a walk in the park.

### Temperament
This is an alert, fearless and happy small terrier, which delights in human company.

### Suitability as a family companion
It is a loving, family dog, small enough to live in a town flat, but equally at home in the country.

### Special needs
Like its cousin, the Norfolk Terrier, this dog hates to be confined to kennels, away from its family.

This is another small, low-to-the-ground terrier from East Anglia. It should be strong and sturdy, with good bone. It has a broad skull, a shortish muzzle, neat, upright ears and dark eyes, all of which combine to give it a bright, alert expression. The body should be compact and sturdy. The tail is carried high, but is customarily docked at the required length.

One of the smallest terriers, the Norwich has much to commend it as a delightful companion and an alert watch-dog.

# OLD ENGLISH SHEEPDOG

*Working group*

**Size**
Males: 55.8 cm (22 ins) and upwards
Females: slightly less
With this breed type, symmetry and character are of greatest importance and should not be sacrificed for size alone.

**Coat**
Profuse, weather-proof, and of good hard texture. It should not be straight, but shaggy and free from curl, with a soft undercoat.

**Colour**
Any shade of grey, grizzle, blue or blue merle, with or without white markings. Any shade of brown or sable is objectionable. Puppies are born black and white and gradually change to their adult coat and colouring by three years.

**Grooming**
With the Old English Sheepdog one must accept the need for regular grooming. Your puppy should be taught to lie on its side while you thoroughly brush and comb, separating any matts with your fingers, and teasing them out. It will also need a bath from time to time, and it is important to make sure it is thoroughly rinsed and dried.

**Exercise**
Besides a regular walk and a gallop in the park, it will also need to have access to a reasonably sized garden.

**Temperament**
Steady and sensible.

**Suitability as a family companion**
One must remember that the attractive cuddly bundle of puppy fun soon grows into a big boisterous dog, needing both grooming and exercise. If you are prepared to cope with this, and teach it good manners, then the breed offers much in return as a hardy, devoted family companion.

**Special needs**
Remember to examine you dog's feet for any lumps of soil or matts between the pads. Also check that the ears are kept clean.

The Old English sheepdog's origins are not clear, but we do know that this large, rough-coated drover dog was used extensively in the west of England and in Wales in the past. The breed became known as the 'bobtail', because of the practice of removing its tail.

It should be a strongly-made, compact dog of great symmetry, free from any legginess. It has a distinctive, low-pitched bark. The jaws are strong, square and fairly long. The head is well covered with hair. The eyes should be dark or wall-eyed and the ears are small.

The body is thick-set and muscular and the hindquarters are strong. The movement is quite distinctive, being very elastic in a gallop and ambling and pacing when it is walking or trotting. The tail is customarily docked.

With correct management from an early age, this dog will grow into a real character.

# PAPILLON

*Toy group*

**Size**
Males and females: 20.3–28 cm (8–11 ins)

**Coat**
The dog has an abundant single coat: long, fine, silky, lying flat with profuse frill on the chest. The back of the front legs, tail and thighs are well-feathered with long hair.

**Colour**
White, with patches which may be any colour except liver. The head markings should be symmetrical with a white, narrow, clearly defined blaze. A tri-colour must be black-and-white with tan spots over the eyes, and tan inside the ears, on cheeks and under root of tail.

**Grooming**
An occasional bath and regular combing keeps the coat in good shape.

**Exercise**
It enjoys outings, but is quite happy in a reasonable-sized garden.

**Temperament**
It is a happy, affectionate, intelligent and gentle dog.

**Suitability as a family companion**
It is a perfect housedog, full of life and animation.

This little dog is surely one of the most beautiful in the toy group. It originated in continental Europe, and used to be a favourite with the nobility.

The skull is slightly rounded and the muzzle finely pointed and abruptly thinner than the skull. The nose should be black and the eyes dark and round.

The ears are an important feature. They may be held erect, in a pose called *Papillon*, or dropped (*Phalene*). They should be large, with rounded tips and heavily fringed. When erect, they must be carried like a butterfly's wings (hence the breed's name).

The body should be well formed, with a deep chest and well sprung ribs. The hindquarters are well developed. The feet are fine, long and hare-like. The long, plumed tail is set on high, arched over the back, with the fringes falling to the side.

# PEKINESE

*Toy group*

**Size**
Males: 5 kg (11 lbs)
Females: 5.5 kg (12 lbs)

**Coat**
Long and straight, with a profuse mane which extends beyond the shoulders, forming a cape or a frill around the neck. The top coat should be rather coarse, and the undercoat should be thick. There should be profuse feathering on the ears, legs, thighs, tail and toes.

**Colour**
All colours and markings are permissible, except liver and albino. Parti-colours should be evenly broken.

**Grooming**
Despite its profuse coat, the Pekinese is not very difficult to keep in good order, provided it has a daily grooming session. Pay special attention to the areas behind the ears and under the

elbows, and to the long trousers. A good down-to-the-skin brush with a pin brush should be fine. If the trousers get dirty, brush them through with talc or grooming powder. Use cotton wool to wipe dry any wetness around the eyes and at the wrinkled nose.

**Exercise**
It is happy in a garden, or with only short walks.

**Temperament**
It is a sporting dog with a lot of personality.

**Suitability as a family companion**
This is the most faithful of companions, and a great character. The Pekinese has been much maligned and is often said to be very yappy. But it is really a sturdy, robust and most delightful dog.

**Special needs**
Apart from its daily groom, this dog also needs to have its nails clipped regularly.

The Pekinese was highly prized as a court dog in ancient China and in the Far East. It first came to Europe in about 1860.

It is a small, well balanced, thick-set dog of great dignity and quality. The head is massive and flat-skulled, with a short nose and large, open nostrils. In profile, the face should look quite flat, with the nose well up between the eyes, which should be large, clear, dark and lustrous. The ears are heart-shaped and covered with long, profuse feathering.

The Pekinese has a distinctive body: short, but with a deep chest. The hindquarters are lighter and lion-like. The back legs are light but firm and well shaped.

The breed should be heavy for its size, but not fat. The tail is set high, carried tightly and slightly curved over the back. The movement is most distinctive: a slow, dignified roll in front, with a close movement behind.

# PHARAOH HOUND

*Hound group*

**Size**
Males: 56–63 cm (22–25 ins)
Females: 52–61 cm (21–24 ins)

**Coat**
Short and glossy, ranging from close
and fine to slightly harsh. There should
be no feathering.

**Colour**
Tan, or rich tan with white markings,
which may only be a white tip to the tail
(very desirable), white on the chest (a
star), white on toes, and a slim white
blaze in centre line of the face. Flecking
or white other than this is undesirable.

**Grooming**
The short coat only requires a good rub
with a hound glove.

**Exercise**
The Pharaoh is a hunting breed that
needs plenty of exercise. It can be
unhappy without it.

**Temperament**
Affectionate and friendly.

**Suitability as a family companion**
The clean lines and neatness of action
make this an appealing pet, which is
good with children. It is not really
suitable as a town dog, where adequate
exercise may be a problem.

**Special needs**
It is a fast hunter of wild rabbits, hares
and game birds, so watch it with stock
that are running loose.

This is a really ancient breed, which has
not changed over the centuries. Its
noble bearing, clean lines and powerful,
free movement all reveal its hunting
background.

The head is wedge-shaped, long and
lean, with the foreface slightly longer
than the skull, and a slight stop. The
jaws should be powerful. The eyes are
oval, amber and with an intelligent
expression. The nose is flesh-coloured
and should blend with the coat, as
should the nails and pads on the feet.

The ears are erect, mobile, fine-
textured and large. The body is lean,
with a deep brisket and well sprung ribs.
The hindquarters are muscular. Strong,
firm, well padded feet are essential.

The tail reaches the hock and should
be fairly thick and tapering. When it
moves, the dog should cover the ground
without any apparent effort.

# POINTER

*Gundog group*

**Size**
Males: 63–69 cm (25–27 ins)
Females: 61–66 cm (24–26 ins)

**Coat**
Short, smooth, straight and fine, with a decided sheen.

**Colour**
The usual colours are lemon-and-white, liver-and-white, orange-and-white, black-and-white. Self colours and tricolours are also correct.

**Grooming**
With its short, fine coat, a good rub with a hound glove keeps it in good fettle.

**Exercise**
This is an active breed that should have unrestricted freedom for exercise to keep it in its best form and condition.

**Temperament**
Biddable and responsive.

**Suitability as a family companion**
This is a contented breed that is affectionate and intelligent. Providing the exercise needs are no problem, the Pointer will fit in well with the household.

**Special needs**
This breed needs quality feeding and space to stretch its limbs when it is growing.

The Pointer should give the appearance of strength, endurance and speed. The head is an important feature. It has a well defined stop, and the skull, of medium length, should balance with the foreface. The nostrils are wide, soft and moist. The muzzle is concave, giving the dog a dish-faced look.

The eyes are brown or hazel, with a slight depression under them.

The general outline from head to tail should be one of graceful curves. The hindquarters are strong. The feet are oval and tight with well padded arched toes. The tail, which is another special feature of the breed, is of medium length, thick at the root and gradually tapering. It should be level with the back and, when the dog is moving, it should lash from side to side. The dog's movement should be smooth with a powerful, driving, hind action.

# POMERANIAN

*Toy group*

**Size**
Males: 1.8–2 kg (4–4.5 lbs)
Females: 2–2.5 kg (4.5–5.5 kg)

**Coat**
Double-coated with soft fluffy
undercoat and a straight, harsh, stand-
off outercoat. The coat is abundant
around the neck, forepart of the
shoulder and chest, and forms a frill.
There is abundant feathering on
hindquarters.

**Colour**
All whole colours are recognized
including sable, wolf and wolf-sable.
White or tan markings are discouraged.
Parti-colours are allowed, but not often
seen. The colours should be evenly
distributed on the body in patches.

**Grooming**
In spite of the Pomeranian's
voluminous coat, it is really extremely
easy to keep in good order. All it needs

is a light, daily brush and a check that
the eyes and ears are clean. It should
have a thorough coat brushing once a
week, getting right down to the skin.

**Exercise**
It will get all the exercise needed in its
own garden and home.

**Temperament**
Alert and amusing, this little dog has
plenty of affection and personality.

**Suitability as a family companion**
Despite its small size, the Pomeranian is
hardy and energetic and makes an
intelligent and charming pet. It has a
long life.

**Special needs**
With all small breeds, special care is
needed when they are young puppies.
But that does not mean they should be
treated as puppies all their lives!

The Pomeranian should be a compact,
sturdy little dog. Its foxy head should be
held high and the dark, oval eyes should
be alert and full of intelligence. The ears
are small, erect and near.

The Pomeranian has a short neck,
and there should be a profuse, lion-like
mane and frill.

The chest should be deep, giving
plenty of heart and lung room. The tail
is a most distinctive feature. It should
be straight and lie absolutely flat along
the back. It is covered with long, thick
hairs that spread out in a beautiful fan.

Anyone seeking a charming and
intelligent dog, but who does not have
the accommodation or energy for a
bigger breed, will find the Pomeranian
ideal. It is an excellent watch-dog, but
take care not to allow it to become a
yapper.

# POODLE

*Utility group*

## Size
The Poodle comes in three sizes.
*Standard:* over 38 cm (15 ins)
*Miniature:* no less than 28 cm (11 ins)
and no more than 38 cm (15 ins)
*Toy:* under 28 cm (11 ins)

## Coat
The coat is very profuse and dense. It
should be of good harsh texture, and
without knots or tangles.

## Colour
All solid colours are permitted.
Whites and creams should have a black
nose, lips, eyerims and toenails.
Browns and café-au-laits have dark
amber eyes, dark liver nose, lips,
eyerims and toenails.
The apricot colour has dark eyes and
black points, or deep amber eyes with
liver points.
The blacks, silvers and blues all have a
black nose, lips, eyerims and toenails.

## Grooming
Professional grooming is really best if
your Poodle is to be kept looking smart.
Although the traditional lion-clip is
adhered to in the show-ring, many easy-
to-manage and attractive trim styles are
available to the pet-owner. Between
trims, a bath and frequent deep-down
brush and comb will keep the tangles
and matts at bay.

## Temperament
Intelligent and full of fun.

## Suitability as a family companion
These have a big advantage: they do not
moult or shed their coats. Their
delightful temperament makes them
excellent companions. The Standard
and Miniatures can be really quite
sporting and are completely at home in
the country or a town house with a
reasonable sized garden. The Toy is fine
for the small house or flat.

All will give much in companionship
and affection and adapt to their owners'
life-style with ease.

The Poodle, in all its three sizes, has
become a popular family dog. At one
time, Toys and Miniatures were
immensely fashionable, and some very
poor specimens were bred. Fortunately,
fashions change and today's owners can
expect high quality in all sizes.

The Poodle is an elegant-looking dog
with a long, fine head. The eyes are
almond-shaped and dark, full of fire
and intelligence. The ears are long and
wide and set low. The chest is deep, and
moderately wide, and the back is strong,
and slightly hollowed. The loins and
thighs are muscular and the feet are
oval and tight with well cushioned pads.
The tail is customarily docked, set on
high, and carried at an angle from the
body: never curled or carried over it.
The Poodle's movement should be light
and springy, with the head and tail
carried high.

Poodles of any size are delightful,
intelligent dogs which are full of fun.
They will repay all the care and
attention needed to keep them looking
and feeling good.

# PUG

*Toy group*

**Size**
Males and females: 6.4–8.2 kg (14–18 lbs)

**Coat**
Smooth, fine, soft, short and glossy. Neither hard nor woolly.

**Colour**
Silver, apricot, fawn or black. The muzzle or mask, ears, moles on cheeks, thumb mark or diamond on the forehead and the trace (a black line extending along the back and neck) should all be clearly defined and as black as possible.

**Grooming**
The short coat presents no problems, and needs only a good, regular brush.

**Exercise**
It enjoys a walk and run in the park, but is equally at home in the garden.

**Temperament**
Good-tempered and intelligent.

**Suitability as a family companion**
This is an excellent family dog, tolerant and adaptable in the home. The Pug is an amusing and delightful character, splendid with children.

**Special needs**
The face folds should be kept clean and free of sores. A little baby oil applied from time to time will be a great help, and also keep the skin supple. With a young puppy, care should be taken that the eyes do not become damaged, either in rough play or on anything protruding.

The Pug is a sturdy, well-built little dog, square and cobby with a wide chest. The head is large, massive and round.

The muzzle is short, square and blunt, but in no way upfaced. The wrinkles are large and deep. The eyes are a great attraction with this breed: they are large, bold and prominent, dark, soft and solicitous in expression. They are very lustrous and full of fire when excited. The tail (or twist) is curled as tightly as possible over the hip. A double curl is considered perfection.

The Pug was popular in Court circles during the time of William and Mary, and has been the devoted pet of royalty and the aristocracy of Europe for centuries, particularly in the reign of George III and in Victorian times.

A unique character, the Pug delights to be one of the family.

# PYRENEAN MOUNTAIN DOG

*Working group*

**Size**
Males: at least 71 cm (28 ins) 50 kg (110 lbs)
Females: at least 66 cm (26 ins) 40 kg (90 lbs)
Great size is essential with this breed.

**Coat**
The topcoat is coarse, thick, straight or slightly wavy, but never curly or fuzzy. There is a profuse undercoat of fine hairs. The coat should be longer around the neck and shoulders (where it forms a mane) and towards the tail. The forelegs are feathered and the hair on the rear of the thighs is long, very dense and more woolly in texture, giving a pantaloon effect.

**Colour**
White or white with patches of wolf-grey or pale yellow, which can be on the head, ears and at the base of the tail. A few patches on the body are also acceptable. It is important the nose and eyerims are black. Liver or pink pigmentation is highly undesirable as are any black patches which go right down to the roots.

**Grooming**
Regular and good brushing and combing are essential for this breed. The effort will be well worthwhile and a splendid looking, noble dog will be the result.

**Exercise**
When it is mature this is a rather lazy breed that does not demand much exercise.

**Temperament**
Placid, amiable and good natured.

**Suitability as a family companion**
This is a big, heavy-coated dog. It can be an affectionate companion and a good friend to the family, to whom it is devoted. It will warn of any unwelcome guests – and keep the right side of the garden fence. It is intelligent and easily trained.

**Special needs**
At eight weeks, the Pyrenean has a lot of growing to do, which means it needs specialized feeding, sensible management and well controlled exercise if it is to grow and thrive properly.

This dog was developed to guard flocks against large animals such as wolves and bears. It is imposing, powerful and very large but, at the same time, it should be elegant and well balanced.

The head should give the impression

of strength. There is almost no stop and the muzzle is strong and slightly tapered. The eyes are dark and intelligent-looking. The ears are fairly small, set level with the eyes and lie flat against the head, but they may be raised when the dog is alert.

The chest is broad and deep and the back long, strong and straight. The loins are muscular and the tail well plumed and thick, tapering towards the tip. It should have a slight curl and be long enough to reach below the hock. It is normally carried low, but is held high when the dog is alert.

The feet are compact and strong, with double dew-claws on the hind legs. The movement is unhurried and ambling.

Despite its large size, the Pyrenean is not really cumbersome. It should not be nervous: take care to choose a puppy with a good temperament.

# RETRIEVER (Curly Coated)

*Gundog group*

**Size**
Males and females: ideally, 63–69 cm (25–27 ins) 31.8–36.3 kg (70–80 lbs)

**Coat**
Waterproof. It should be a mass of crisp, small, tight curls all over. This is the main characteristic of the breed.

**Colour**
Black or liver.

**Grooming**
This dog is not brushed and combed. Instead, the coat is dampened and then rubbed over with a cloth to take off the dirt. After that, use your flat bare hand and massage it in a circular movement. This will help keep the curls tight.

**Exercise**
This is a strong active breed that needs plenty of exercise.

**Temperament**
Sweet natured, faithful and friendly.

**Suitability as a family companion**
This is a gundog with a sense of fun. It is friendly and can be a good family dog as well as a good guard.

**Special needs**
This dog can be a little headstrong and needs firm, understanding management.

The 'Curly Coat' has a long, well proportioned head, with a flat skull and a long, strong jaw. The eyes are large and black and the ears are set low, close to the head and are covered with short curls.

The body has good depth of brisket, well sprung ribs and is not too long in the loin. The hindquarters are muscular. The feet are round and compact, with well arched toes. The tail, which is covered with curls, is moderately short, tapers towards a point and is carried fairly straight.

This dog is squarely built and particularly good in water. It has a great sense of humour, a natural working ability and a willing response to training.

# RETRIEVER (Flat Coat)

*Gundog group*

**Size**
Males and females: 27.2–31.8 kg (60–70 lbs)

**Coat**
Flat, dense, of fine quality and texture.

**Colour**
Black or liver.

**Grooming**
It is easy to groom: a good regular brush several times a week keeps the coat gleaming.

**Exercise**
A good working breed that needs regular exercise.

**Temperament**
Bright and active.

**Suitability as a family companion**
This is a sensible dog, not very demanding, and it is very good with children.

**Special needs**
This dog likes to be occupied, but it is not destructive.

This medium-sized British breed is intelligent and teachable. It owes its origins to the Setter and the Newfoundland.

The head should be long and nicely moulded, the skull flat and moderately broad. The nose should be a good size, with open nostrils and strong jaws.

The eyes are dark brown or hazel, medium-sized and very intelligent-looking. The ears are small and lie close to the head. The chest is deep and fairly broad.

The hindquarters are muscular and the hindlegs and tail nicely feathered, well set on and carried gaily, but never much above the level of the back. The pads should be thick and strong and the feet round, with close, well arched toes.

# RETRIEVER (Golden)

*Gundog group*

**Size**
Males: 56–61 cm (22–24 ins) 32–37 kg
(70–80 lbs)
Females: 51–56 cm (20–22 ins) 27–32 kg
(60–70 lbs)

**Coat**
Flat or wavy, with good feathering and
a dense, water-resisting undercoat.

**Colour**
Any shade of gold or cream, but neither
red nor mahogany. A few white hairs in
the chest are permissible.

**Grooming**
Regular grooming with a bush and
comb is essential, but no problem.

**Exercise**
With its origins as a working gundog,
plenty of exercise is a must for this
breed.

**Temperament**
It has a most kind and intelligent
disposition.

**Suitability as a family companion**
With its kind expression and delightful
disposition, the Golden Retriever is
splendid as a family dog. It is easy to
train and it loves to please.

**Special needs**
Do not let it get too fat.

The Golden Retriever was first bred in
Scotland on the estate of the first Lord
Tweedmouth. It was later taken up by
other enthusiasts.

This is a symmetrical, active and
powerful dog. It has a broad skull with
a powerful muzzle and a good stop. The
eyes are dark, with dark rims. They are
set well apart, and have a kindly
expression.

The body should be well balanced,
with plenty of heart and lung room. The
ribs are well sprung and the
hindquarters are strong and muscular.
The feet should be round and cat-like.
The tail is well feathered, carried level
with the back.

This breed has a good life-span, and
will be a loving, loyal and devoted
member of the family.

# RETRIEVER (Labrador)

*Gundog group*

**Size**
Males: 56–57 cm (22–22.5 ins)
Females: 54–56 cm (21.5–22 ins)

**Coat**
The coat is a distinctive feature of the breed. It should be short and dense, without wave. The undercoat should be weather-resisting.

**Colour**
Black, yellow, chocolate.

**Grooming**
It should have regular brush and comb, especially when moulting, and good wipe over with a chamois leather.

**Exercise**
It should have daily good brisk walk and/or free run, or both.

**Temperament**
A bright and happy disposition. This dog likes to be occupied.

**Suitability as a family companion**
This is the most popular of the Retriever breeds. It has great appeal for its all-round ability and intelligence. It is a really splendid family dog.

**Special needs**
It can be quite greedy and will eat anything. Take care to feed it adequately but do not overfeed.

Compared with some breeds, the Labrador is quite new. It originated in Newfoundland. Nowadays, they are used as gundogs, drug detectors, guide dogs and family pets.

The Labrador is a strongly built dog. It has a clean-cut head, broad and with a pronounced stop. The jaws are powerful. The eyes are medium-sized, dark brown or hazel and should express intelligence and good temper. The ears are set rather far back.

The breed should have a body of good depth, with well sprung ribs. The hindquarters should be well developed.

The tail should be otter-like, thick at the root and tapering. It is quite flat on the underside and covered with short, thick, dense hair, giving it a rounded appearance.

# RHODESIAN RIDGEBACK

*Hound group*

**Size**
Males: 63–68 cm (25–27 ins) 36.3 kg (80 lbs)
Females: 61–66 cm (24–26 ins) 31.7 kg (70 lbs)

**Coat**
Short and dense, sleek and glossy. It should be neither woolly nor silky.

**Colour**
Light wheaten to red-wheaten. A little white on the chest and toes is permissible, but excessive white is undesirable.

**Grooming**
Grooming and general care presents no problem with this short-coated breed. All it needs is a good brush twice a week.

**Exercise**
This is a hunting breed that should be capable of great endurance and a fair amount of speed. It must have adequate exercise.

**Temperament**
Faithful and gentle.

**Suitability as a family companion**
This handsome upstanding breed proves a good guard, and a faithful family dog.

**Special needs**
Like most hunting dogs, it does need plenty of exercise. Apart from this, it presents no problems.

The Ridgeback, developed in Southern Africa, was known as the 'lion-dog'. It was not used to attack lions, but rather to track and harass them, making them easy targets for the hunters.

This is a muscular dog with a distinctive ridge of hair along the centre of the back, running from immediately behind the shoulder to the hip bones. It must contain two identical crowns of hair, about 5 cm (2 ins) wide.

The head is fairly long and the muzzle deep and powerful, with tight lips. The nose is black or brown, depending on the coat colour. The eyes also harmonize with the dog's colour.

The ears are close to the head, set up rather high and of medium size. The chest should be deep and the front legs well boned, muscular and straight. The tail is gently tapering and is carried with a slight upward curve.

# ROTTWEILER

*Working group*

**Size**
Males: ideally 63.5–68.5 cm (25–27 ins)
Females: ideally 58.4–63.5 cm (23–25 ins)

**Coat**
Medium-long, coarse and flat with an undercoat.

**Colour**
Black, with clearly defined rich tan to mahogany-brown markings on the cheeks, muzzle, chest and legs as well as over both eyes and the area beneath the tail.

**Grooming**
A regular good brush and comb.

**Exercise**
Once a drovers' dog, adequate exercise is important.

**Temperament**
Very intelligent, bold and courageous.

**Suitability as a family companion**
It needs firm handling when it is young.

**Special needs**
It is essential to appreciate the need for really good feeding and sensible rearing. Do not over-exercise it as an adolescent.

This dog gets its name from the town of Rottweil, in southern Germany. It is a larger-than-medium-sized breed with a compact, well proportioned frame. The head is broad, with a pronounced stop. The muzzle is fairly deep and the cheeks are well muscled. The skin on the head may show some wrinkle when the dog is attentive. The nose is always black and the eyes are dark brown and almond-shaped. The ears are set high.

The back should be straight and firm and the hindquarters broad and well muscled. The feet are round and compact. The tail is customarily docked and should not be set too low. When moving, the Rottweiler should look harmonious and unrestricted, giving the impression of supple strength. A Rottweiler should never look timid or stupid. Its owner should take time to let it develop its full potential.

# SAINT BERNARD

*Working group*

### Size
Males: at least 69 cm (27.5 ins)
Females: at least 65 cm (25.5 ins), finer
and more delicate than the male.
The breed standard states that the taller
the dog is, the better, as long as
symmetry is maintained. The breed
should be well proportioned and of
great substance.

### Coat
*Smooth:* the coat should be very dense
and lying close. It should be tough,
without feeling rough. There is slight
feathering on the thighs and tail.
*Rough:* the coat is of medium length,
dense and rough. It is rather fuller
around the neck. There is slight
feathering on the front legs and the
thighs are well feathered. The tail has
dense hair of medium length. The coat
should never be curly or shaggy.

### Colour
The colours should be orange,
mahogany-brindle, red-brindle (in
various shades with white). The
markings should be a white muzzle,
white blaze on the face, white collar,
chest, forelegs, feet and end of tail and
black shadings on the face and ears. The
white on the end of the tail is similar to
the requirements with some hound
breeds.

### Grooming
A daily good grooming is a must. Pay
particular attention to the hair behind
the ears and side of the neck, which can
get matted.

### Exercise
It is not overdemanding with its needs,
and prefers a short comfortable walk to
something long or strenuous.

### Temperament
Benevolent and intelligent.

### Suitability as a family companion
This is rather a large dog for the
modern home. Although it usually has a
good disposition, it may not always be
as mild-mannered as one might imagine.

### Special needs
A Saint Bernard has a big frame, and
will grow to be very large. It will need
really good feeding, with calcium
additives when it is young and growing.
It tends to slobber and can be a messy
feeder.

This is a Colossus of a dog – a symbol
of strength and sacrifice. The tales of its
heroism in its native Alps are legendary.

Its head is massive: the muzzle is
short and square. The nose should be
large and black, with well developed
nostrils. The eyes are rather small, deep-
set and dark. The lower eyelid droops,
so as to show a fair amount of haw. As
one might expect from the traditional
role of the Saint Bernard, and the
environment it comes from, its body is
deep and muscular, with a broad,
straight back and powerful loins. The
neck is thick and strong.

The feet are large and compact, with
well arched toes. The hindquarters
should be muscular and well developed.

Take care to choose a puppy that has
been well reared and avoid one that is
over-wrinkled in the skull, as this can
lead to eye problems later.

# SALUKI

*Hound group*

**Size**
Males: 58–71 cm (28 ins)
Females: proportionately smaller

**Coat**
*Smooth*: the coat is soft and silky.
*Feathered*: there is feathering on the back of the legs and thighs.

**Colour**
Any colour is permissible.

**Grooming**
A good rub over with the hound glove is usually sufficient.

**Exercise**
It needs to be given adequate free exercise.

**Temperament**
Gentle and faithful.

**Suitability as a family companion**
This sensitive breed becomes very attached to the family and makes an excellent companion. It is clean in its habits, has no doggy odour, and is quiet and gentle about the house.

**Special needs**
This breed can be somewhat nervous, so it is important to look for a puppy with an outgoing temperament. It also likes to dig in the garden, so it needs to be watched for this. It becomes bored if it is left alone for long periods.

The Saluki, also known as the Gazelle Hound, is said to be the oldest domesticated pure breed in the world. It is thought to have originated as a hunting dog in Syria. The Crusaders brought the breed to Europe in the Middle Ages.

It should be graceful, strong and very fast. The head is long and narrow, with a black or liver nose. The eyes are dark to hazel, large and oval. They should have a dignified expression: deep, gentle and far-seeing. The ears are close to the skull and are long and mobile, with silky hair.

The neck should be long, supple and well muscled, while the chest is deep and quite narrow. The back is broad and the hindquarters should show power. The feet are long and supple, with long toes. The tail is low set and carried in a curve. It should be feathered on the underside, with long silky hair.

The Saluki is affectionate with its owner, but aloof with strangers. It does not demand attention and, in the right home, it is a really splendid and clean house dog.

# SAMOYED

*Working group*

**Size**
Males: 50.8–55.8 cm (20–22 ins)
Females: 45.7–50.8 cm (18–20 ins)

**Coat**
The body should be well covered with a thick, close, soft and short undercoat, with harsh hair growing through it forming the outer coat. This should stand straight away from the body and be free from curl.

**Colour**
Pure white, white-and-biscuit, cream.

**Grooming**
With its heavy coat, this dog needs a regular and deep brush and comb.

**Exercise**
This was a herding and sledge dog, and adequate and sensible exercise is important for it.

**Temperament**
Intelligent, affectionate and companionable.

**Suitability as a family companion**
This is one of the oldest known breeds. It is rarely a trouble-maker; it is good with children and is an excellent watch-dog.

**Special needs**
The Samoyed can be vocal, so it should be trained not to be. It really does need regular grooming.

The Samoyed should be strong and graceful as well as hardy, intelligent and active. It originates in a cold climate, and should therefore have a good, heavy, weather-resisting coat. The head is powerful and wedge-shaped, with a broad, flat skull and a medium-length muzzle. The eyes are almond-shaped, medium to dark brown and set well apart, with an alert, intelligent expression. The body is muscular and flexible, and the dog should look capable of great endurance. The chest is deep, with well sprung ribs and a strong, arched neck.

The feet should be flattish and slightly spread out. The tail is long and profuse and carried over the back when alert. It is usually dropped when the dog is at rest.

# SCHIPPERKE

*Utility group*

**Size**
Males and females: 5.4–7.2 kg (12–16 lbs)

**Coat**
Abundant and slightly harsh to the touch, shorter on the ears, muzzle and legs with distinctive ruff and cape around the neck and good culottes on the back of the thighs.

**Colour**
Mainly black or golden. Other whole colours are rare, but they are allowed.

**Grooming**
Its grooming needs are straightforward: just a regular good brush and comb.

**Exercise**
It does not need a great deal of exercise, but it will enjoy all it gets and still be ready for more.

**Temperament**
A happy, hardy, active small dog, which can be somewhat vocal.

**Suitability as a family companion**
The Schipperke makes a splendid family and watch-dog. It is at home in the town or a flat or the country.

The Schipperke (pronounced *skipper-key*) originated on the canal barges in Belgium and Holland. It is an excellent watch-dog, and hunter of vermin, and can also be frisky and entertaining. It is always interested in all that goes on around it.

It is small and cobby, with a thick-set body and deep chest with somewhat lighter hindquarters. The back is straight and the tail customarily docked. The head is fairly broad and fox-like, with dark brown, small, oval eyes, not full, but bright and full of expression. The ears are neat and upright. The coat is weather-resistant and not long enough to be troublesome.

Being an intelligent dog, the Schipperke likes to be occupied and it is extremely loyal to its owner.

# SCHNAUZER

**Size**
*Standard* (or *Medium*)
Males: 48 cm (19 ins)
Females: a little smaller
*Miniature*
Males: 35 cm (14 ins)
Females: a little smaller

**Coat**
A harsh wiry outer coat, and dense soft undercoat. It has a prominent beard and eyebrows.

**Colour**
Either solid black or the unique pepper-and-salt, which fades into a light grey or silvery-white on the eyebrows, cheeks, beard, under the throat, on the chest, legs and under the tail. The pepper-and-salt colouring is shades of grey with individual hairs banded light-dark-light, interspersed with darker guard hairs. The colour can vary from a light silver-grey through to dark steel depending on the depth and colouring of the banding. Miniatures also have the added attraction of the black and silver colour which follows the same pattern as the pepper-and-salts except that the main colour is solid black.

**Grooming**
The Schnauzer breeds, whatever their size, are enhanced by correct and regular grooming. Their coats are easy to manage, and most people are quickly able to master the art of keeping their pet neat and tidy. The standard size usually has the more manageable coat. Regular scraping with a stripping knife to remove the full soft undercoat will help keep the coat more manageable.

**Exercise**
This is a contented and adaptable breed. It does not need a tremendous amount of exercise, but does enjoy it.

**Temperament**
Happy, intelligent and companionable, this dog is amenable to training and devoted to its family.

**Suitability as a family companion**
This is primarily a companion dog and an excellent watch-dog. It is sensible and adaptable, fine with children and an ideal family dog.

**Special needs**
The Schnauzer has a non-shed coat but needs regular grooming to prevent matts and tangles. With the Miniatures, hair may need to be pulled from the ears from time to time.

The Schnauzer originated in Bavaria, several centuries ago. It was used for ratting, droving and as a watch-dog. Miniature Schnauzers came later.

It is a very nearly square dog, being balanced and sturdy. The head is a distinguishing feature. It should be elongated, with a powerful muzzle. The beard and eyebrows are prominent. The eyes are dark and full of character. The ears should be neat and 'V'-shaped.

The body is roomy and the chest deep. The back is firm and the tail, which is customarily docked, is carried erect. The coat is harsh and wiry, with harsher hair on the legs. The furnishings are fairly thick, but not silky. The movement should be free-flowing and rhythmic.

With the Schnauzer breeds, emphasis has always been on a functional utilitarian dog with character.

# SCOTTISH TERRIER

*Terrier group*

**Size**
Males and females: 25.4–28 cm (10–11 ins) 8.6–10.4 kg (19–23 lbs)

**Coat**
Short and weather-resisting, with a dense, soft undercoat and a harsh, dense, wiry outer coat.

**Colour**
Black, wheaten or brindle of any colour.

**Grooming**
Like all trimmed breeds, the 'Scottie' needs regular and proper coat care. It should be stripped at least twice a yer. The puppy will soon get used to and enjoy regular attention and trimming sessions.

**Exercise**
Despite its short legs, this dog thoroughly enjoys regular walks and a free run in the park. It is also content with just being able to run around the house and garden.

**Temperament**
This is an outgoing terrier that can sometimes be obstinate and strong-willed.

**Suitability as a family companion**
The Scottie is a most suitable family dog, loyal and devoted to its family.

**Special needs**
It should have firm handling from the start.

Originally called the Aberdeen Terrier, this dog became known as the Scottish Terrier towards the end of the 1880s. It has kept the name ever since.

This is a sturdy, thickset dog which suggests great power and activity in a small compass. The head should look long for a dog of this size, but it should still be in proportion to the body. The nose should be large, the eyes are almond-shaped and dark. They are fairly far apart and set deeply under the eyebrows. The ears are neat, pointed and erect.

The body should be muscular and sturdy, with a well rounded rib cage. The hindquarters should be powerful and the tail short and thick at the root. It is carried upright.

The Scottie is good with children and other pets and is a splendid, robust companion, with lots of style.

# SEALYHAM TERRIER

*Terrier group*

**Size**
Males: no more than 30 cm (12 ins) 9 kg (20 lbs)
Females: no more than 30 cm (12 ins) 8 kg (18 lbs)

**Coat**
The topcoat is long, hard and wiry. The undercoat is dense.

**Colour**
Mostly white, or white with brown, lemon or badger-pied markings on the head and eyes.

**Grooming**
It is important the coat is groomed every day and not allowed to get out of hand. The Sealyham needs trimming at least twice a year, with patience and following the correct pattern. The results can be most rewarding if you do it yourself.

**Exercise**
This is a strongly built, low-to-the-ground, active dog which enjoys exercising in a fairly large garden.

**Temperament**
It is somewhat self-willed and obstinate, so it needs to know from an early age who is boss.

**Suitability as a family companion**
It needs a family who will understand the breed's need for careful coat care and its strong will.

Originating in Sealyham, Wales, some hundred years ago, this short-legged terrier was created to be an excellent hunter above and below the ground.

The Sealyham has a strong head, with a slightly domed skull and strong jaws. The eyes are dark, round and of medium size. The ears are slightly rounded and carried at the side of the cheek.

Well boned, the breed has a flexible body of medium length with a deep broad chest well let down between the front legs, strong hindquarters and a level back. The tail is customarily docked and carried high.

The Sealyham has lots to offer but does need firm handling.

# SHETLAND SHEEPDOG

*Working group*

**Size**
Males: 37 cm (14.5 ins)
Females: 35.5 ins (14 ins)

**Coat**
The coat must be double. The outercoat is long, of harsh texture and straight. The undercoat is soft, short and close. The mane and frill should be very abundant and forelegs well feathered. The hindlegs above the hocks are profusely covered with hair, but below the hocks they are fairly smooth.

**Colour**
Tricolours: these should be an intense black on the body, with no signs of ticking. Rich tan markings are preferred.
    Sables: these may be clear or shaded, any colour from gold to deep mahogany, but in its shade the colour should be rich in tones. Wolf-sable and grey are undesirable.
    Blue merles: these should be a clear silvery blue, splashed and marbled with black. Rich tan markings to be preferred but the absence not to be counted as a fault. Heavy black markings, slate-coloured or rusty tinge in either top or undercoat are highly undesirable. The general effect should be blue. White markings may be shown in the blaze, collar, chest, frill, legs,

stifle and tip of the tail.
    All or some tan markings may be shown on eyebrows, cheeks, legs, stifles and under the tail. All or some of the white markings are preferred whatever the colour of the dog, but their absence shall not be considered a fault. Black-and-white and black-and-tan are also-recognized colours. Over-markings of patches of white on the body are highly undesirable. The nose should be black, whatever the colour of the dog.

**Grooming**
A clean dog by nature, the Shetland Sheepdog is not difficult to groom. It does not require the attention to its coat that one would perhaps imagine. A good deep down brush and comb two or three times a week most of the year, and daily at moulting time, will be fine.

**Exercise**
This is an active breed that enjoys its walks and free run in the park or field.

**Temperament**
It has a pleasant nature, it is intelligent, but can be a little stubborn. Somewhat reserved towards strangers. Avoid a puppy that is shy and retiring.

**Suitability as a family companion**
This is a handsome breed. It is a handy size and is loyal and affectionate to its owner and household.

The Shetland resembles the Rough Collie. It should be strong and active-looking, free from any coarseness.
    The head should be wedge-shaped, with a flat skull and a well defined stop. The skull and muzzle should be of equal length. The eyes are almond-shaped and set obliquely. They are usually brown, except for merles, where they may be blue. The ears are small, fairly wide at the base and set close together, high up on the skull. In repose, they are thrown back, but when alert they should be brought forward and carried erect, with the tips dropping forward. These features all combine to give the dog an expression of alert, gentle intelligence.
    The body is slightly longer than it is high, with a deep chest and well sprung ribs. The tail is set low and must reach the hock joint. It should be abundantly feathered. The action should be lithe and graceful.
    This is one of the beauties of the canine world, and is a more natural, sturdy and trouble-free breed than it may at first look.

# SIBERIAN HUSKY

*Working group*

**Size**
Males: 53–60 cm (21–23.5 ins) 20–27 kg
(45–60 lbs)
Females: 51–56 cm (20–22 ins) 16–23 kg
(35–50 lbs)

**Coat**
It has a double coat of medium length,
but which should never be so long as to
obscure the clean-cut outline of the dog.
It should give a well-furred appearance.
The undercoat is soft and dense.

**Colour**
All colours including white, and all
shapes and sizes of markings are
permissible.

**Grooming**
These dogs are remarkably clean, and

groom themselves like cats. The coat
needs little attention except a good
brush.

**Exercise**
Plenty of exercise is essential.

**Temperament**
Friendly, gentle, outgoing and alert.

**Suitability as a family companion**
This dog is affectionate and gentle with
children, though it is also reserved and
dignified. It is not unduly suspicious of
strangers or aggressive with other dogs.
It is a striking breed that makes a good
family dog.

**Special needs**
This breed adjusts well to indoor living,
but owners must be prepared to give it
the exercise it needs.

Siberian Huskies originated among the
nomadic tribes of Siberia, who kept
them as pets as well as working dogs.
The breed combines a good
temperament with hardiness and
stamina. The body proportions should
reflect a balance of power, speed and
endurance. The movement is smooth,
and seems effortless.

The head is of medium size and the
ears are erect, set close together and
well furred. The eyes are almond-shaped
and may be any shade of blue or brown.
It is quite common for a dog to have an
eye of each colour or even to have a
parti-coloured eye.

The neck is strong and of medium
length. The tail is well furred and
carried over the back in a graceful sickle
curve when attentive. It may trail when
the dog is working or in repose.

# SKYE TERRIER

*Terrier group*

**Size**
Males: 25.4 cm (10 ins) 11.3. kg (25 lbs)
Females: slightly smaller

**Coat**
It is double-coated with a long, hard, harsh, straight topcoat, lying flat and free from curl. The undercoat is short, close, soft and woolly. The coat of the puppy may vary considerably from that of an adult.

**Colour**
Dark or light grey, fawn, cream (all with black points), and black. In fact any self colour is allowed, allowing for shading of the same colour and a lighter undercoat, providing the nose and ears are black. A small white spot on the chest is permissible.

**Grooming**
Regular grooming is essential to keep the coat in good condition.

**Exercise**
This is a great working terrier and it needs to be given a reasonable amount of exercise. It enjoys a free run in the park.

**Temperament**
A one-person dog, somewhat distrustful of strangers. Avoid a shy or aggressive puppy.

**Suitability as a family companion**
At one time, this was a popular terrier, but fashions have changed and it is not so well-known today. However, it still has its followers, and it is better-tempered than it used to be.

This is one of the oldest breeds. It gets its name from the Isle of Skye, where it has always been a working terrier, used for hunting among rocks on dry land and in the water.

The head is long, with powerful jaws and dark brown, close-set eyes, full of expression. The ears are either prick or dropped and gracefully feathered.

The body is long and low, with a level back and a deep chest. The front legs are short and muscular and well angulated. The feet are large and pointed. The tail is long and should be well feathered and carried above the level of the back only when the dog is excited. The dog's movement should be free, active and effortless.

This fascinating old breed is a real working terrier: fearless, loyal and canny. It has lots of style and dignity and is friendly with those it knows.

# SOFT-COATED WHEATEN TERRIER

*Terrier group*

**Size**
Males: 45.7–49.5 cm (18–19.5 ins) 15.9–20.4 kg (35–45 lbs)
Females: slightly less

**Coat**
Soft and silky. It can be loosely waved, or have large, loose light curls. The coat should not be woolly or wiry, nor should it stand off. It should flow or fall naturally. It does not shed.

**Colour**
It should be a good, clear shade of wheaten, like ripening wheat.

**Grooming**
It should not be over-timed or stylized. All it needs is a regular brush and good deep-down comb to keep the tangles out, plus a tidy round the feet.

**Exercise**
This dog is happy with or without a great deal of exercise.

**Temperament**
Good-tempered, spirited and game. This is not an aggressive terrier and does not seek a fight, although it can take care of itself it it needs to.

**Suitability as a family companion**
This dog will appeal to anyone seeking a natural breed that is game and intelligent. It is not over-demanding, is good with children, and is an affectionate, adaptable companion and guard. It suits either town or country life.

The Wheaten is an old Irish breed from County Kerry. It was used to herd farm animals, kill vermin and as a companion and watchdog. It is a natural terrier with a strong, hardy constitution.

A medium-sized breed, the head is moderately long and powerful, with strong jaws and a square muzzle. The stop is well-defined. The nose is black and the hazel eyes are clear and bright, set under a strong brow. The ears are 'V'-shaped, thin, fairly small and fold at the level of the skull.

The front legs are straight, and the body is powerful with hindquarters that are strong and muscular. The feet are compact with deep pads. The tail is customarily docked, set on high and carried gaily, but never over the back. The movement should be well co-ordinated with a good reach in front and a good drive behind.

# SPANIEL, AMERICAN COCKER

*Gundog group*

**Size**
Males: 38 cm (15 ins)
Females: 35 cm (14 ins)

**Coat**
Medium-length, silky and flat or slightly wavy, with enough undercoat to give protection. The ears, chest, abdomen and legs should be well feathered, but not so much as to hide its true lines or affect its function as a sporting dog. The coat should not be too cottony or curly.

**Colour**
Black, buff or any solid colour, as well as black-and-tan, tricolours or parti-colours.

**Grooming**
The coat needs a lot of attention, with frequent combing and brushing right to the skin and the occasional good bath. The head should be trimmed and generally kept tidy. If proper care is not given, the coat will look unkempt, with matts and tangles.

**Temperament**
This is a merry, effervescent and equable dog.

**Suitability as a family companion**
The American Cocker adapts easily to family life, and is very good with children.

As its name implies, this dog was developed in America, though its origins lie with the English Cocker Spaniel. It is a glamorous dog, ideal for the show ring.

The head should be rounded with a pronounced stop. The muzzle is broad and deep, with square, even jaws. In the blacks and black-and-tans, the nose should be black. In the reds, buffs, livers and parti-colours it may be black or brown, with the darker colour preferred. The eyes are slightly almond-shaped. The expression is alert, soft and appealing. The well feathered ears are set no higher than the lower part of the eye and should reach to the muzzle.

The body is short and firm, with wide hips and muscular quarters. The pads should be deep and tough with round, firm feet. The tail is customarily docked and is carried in line with the back or slightly higher.

# SPANIEL, BRITTANY

*Gundog group*

**Size**
Males and females: 44.4–52 cm (17.5–20.5 ins) 13.6–18.2 kg (30–40 lbs)

**Coat**
Dense and either flat or wavy (never curly or silky). The furnishings are not profuse.

**Colour**
Dark orange and white, or liver and white. Some ticking is desirable, but not too much.

**Grooming**
The coat is easy to manage and needs only a regular, good brush and comb.

**Exercise**
This breed is vigorous and energetic and needs a good run or walk daily.

**Temperament**
Sensitive and responsive.

**Suitability as a family companion**
The Brittany is a splendid breed for a family either in the town or the country: it is a handy size and has a responsive temperament as well as a sensible coat, without too much in the way of furnishings.

This is a fast, tireless worker in all sorts of terrain. It has a good sense of smell.

It should look elegant and compact: rugged without being clumsy. The head is of medium length, with a well defined but gently sloping stop. The muzzle tapers gently. The nose should be fawn or tan, eyes dark and expressive. The ears are set above the level of the eye. They should be covered with dense, short hair and should have a little fringe.

The square body should have a good deep chest with plenty of heart and lung room. The back is strong and the hindquarters are broad, strong and muscular. The feet have thick pads and well arched toes. The breed may be either tailless, or have its tail docked short. The dog should move energetically and with purpose.

# SPANIEL, CAVALIER KING CHARLES

*Toy group*

**Size**
Males and females: 5.4–8.2 kg (12–18 lbs)

**Coat**
The coat is long, silky and free from curl. A slight wave is permissible. There should be plenty of feather.

**Colour**
Black-and-tan: raven black with bright tan markings above the eyes, on the cheeks, inside the ears, on the chest and legs and on the underside of the tail. Ruby: a whole-coloured rich red. Blenheim: rich chestnut markings well broken up on a pearly white ground, leaving room between the ears for the unique characteristic of the breed: the much-valued lozenge mark or spot.

Tri-colour: black and white, well spaced and broken up, with tan markings over the eyes, on the cheeks, inside the ears, inside the legs and under the tail.

**Grooming**
The breed requires an occasional bath using a mild dog shampoo and a regular good brush and comb and rub over with a cloth.

**Exercise**
Enjoys a good walk and run in the park.

**Temperament**
Bright and fearless.

**Suitability as a family companion**
The Cavalier is excellent as a family companion. It is adaptable, and well suited to a town or country life and is especially good with children.

The Cavalier King Charles Spaniel is a direct descendant of the small toy spaniels commonly kept by court ladies of Tudor times.

The breed should look active, graceful and well balanced. The body should be short-coupled with plenty of spring in the rib. The back should be level and the head almost flat between the ears. The muzzle is tapered.

The eyes are dark, not prominent, round and spaced well apart. The ears should be long, set high, with plenty of feather. The feet are compact, cushioned and also well feathered. The tail may be docked, but this is optional and no more than one third should be removed. The breed should be very free in action.

This is a hardy, glamorous and companionable breed, which should not be in any way nervous or delicate.

# SPANIEL, CLUMBER

*Gundog group*

**Size**
Males: 42.5–45 cm (17–18 ins) 25–31.8
kg (55–70 lbs)
Females: 42.5–45 cm (17–18 ins) 20.4–
27.2 kg (45–60 lbs)

**Coat**
Abundant, close, silky and straight,
with well feathered legs.

**Colour**
Plain white, with lemon markings.
Orange is permissible. Slight head
markings and a flecked muzzle with
white body are preferred.

**Grooming**
A rub with the hound glove and a comb
through the furnishings is fine.

**Exercise**
It is not very demanding. A good walk
and the chance of a free run will keep
your Clumber in good shape.

**Temperament**
Active, thoughtful and kind.

**Suitability as a family companion**
Easily trained, the Clumber remembers
its lessons well, even if it is only
occasionally used as a sporting dog. The
Clumber is perhaps best for a country
home.

**Special needs**
A young Clumber needs good feeding,
with some additives. The eyes can be
something of a problem, so do not
choose a puppy with a too heavily-
wrinkled head.

The Clumber gets its name from
Clumber in Nottinghamshire, the estate
of the Duke of Newcastle. It was
developed to work in dense
undergrowth. It is a short-legged, large-
bodied Spaniel, with a characteristic,
rolling gait.
 The head is massive: broad on top,
with heavy brows and a deep stop. The
muzzle is heavy and the flews well
developed. The nose is square and flesh-
coloured. The eyes are dark amber and
slightly sunk.
 The front legs are thick, straight and
strong. The body is heavy with well
sprung ribs, a deep chest and a straight,
broad back. The hindquarters are
powerful and the feet round, large and
well covered with hair. The tail is set
low, well feathered and carried level
with the back. It is customarily docked.

# SPANIEL, COCKER

*Gundog group*

**Size**
Males: 39–41 cm (15.5–16 ins) 12.7–14.5 kg (28–32 lbs)
Females: 38–39 cm (15–15.5 cm) 12.7–14.5 kg (28–32 lbs)

**Coat**
Flat and silky, never wiry or wavy. There should be sufficient feather, not too profuse, and never curly.

**Colour**
The colours come in a wide range. The most popular are black, blue-roan, golden, blues, black-and-white, orange-and-white and tri-coloured.

**Grooming**
This breed needs trimming to keep the correct shape and outline as well as a good daily brush and comb. When kept in good order it looks splendid.

**Exercise**
It enjoys walks, and the chance of a good run in a field or park.

**Temperament**
It has a happy, merry nature.

**Suitability as a family companion**
The Cocker is one of the most popular dogs and it makes a splendid family pet. It is affectionate and lively and enjoys life with a family. It is good with children and is a responsive sporting dog.

The Cocker is a sporting dog, small enough to move easily among briars and brambles in all kinds of terrain. It has a good nose: it is untiring and returns game well. It likes to please, so encouragement and a kind voice will produce the best results.

The head should be well balanced with a distinct stop. The muzzle is square and equal in length to the skull. The full, dark eyes should have a gentle, intelligent expression. The ears are set on low, level with the eyes and should not extend beyond the nose. They are covered with long, straight, silky hair.

The body should be strong and the chest is well developed. There should be feathering on the front legs and above the hocks of the hind legs. The hindquarters are wide and muscular. The feet are firm and cat-like. The tail is customarily docked and is set on slightly lower than the line of the back.

This is a popular breed, so it is especially important to make sure you get your puppy from a reliable breeder.

# SPANIEL, ENGLISH SPRINGER

*Gundog group*

**Size**
Males and females: 51 cm (20 ins) 22.7 kg (50 lbs)

**Coat**
Close, straight and weather-resisting, without being coarse.

**Colour**
Usually liver-and-white or black-and-white, or either of these colours with tan markings preferred.

**Grooming**
There are no problems with this breed. A good rub over with the hound glove or a brush and then comb through the furnishings will be enough.

**Exercise**
This is an active breed that needs a fair amount of sensible exercise and the opportunity for a good free run.

**Temperament**
Gentle and friendly.

**Suitability as a family companion**
This dog is good with children and willing to join in their activities. It fits in well with family life, but is better suited to the country than to the town.

The Springer has been around for a very long time. It is built to find and retrieve game throughout a long day, even in the roughest countryside.

It is medium-sized and is the tallest of the land Spaniels. The skull is of medium length, with the foreface proportionate to the skull. The eyes should be dark hazel, medium-sized and should not show any haw. The ears are lobe-shaped.

The body should be strong, with good chest room, well sprung ribs and broad, muscular thighs. The feet are round and compact with full pads. The tail is customarily docked. It should never be carried above the level of the back.

The Springer's movement is smooth and effortless with the forelegs swinging straight forward from the shoulder in a free and easy manner, with the hindlegs driving powerfully.

This is every inch a sporting dog, with a lovely, soft, gentle expression. It combines beauty with stylish and enthusiastic working ability.

# SPANIEL, FIELD

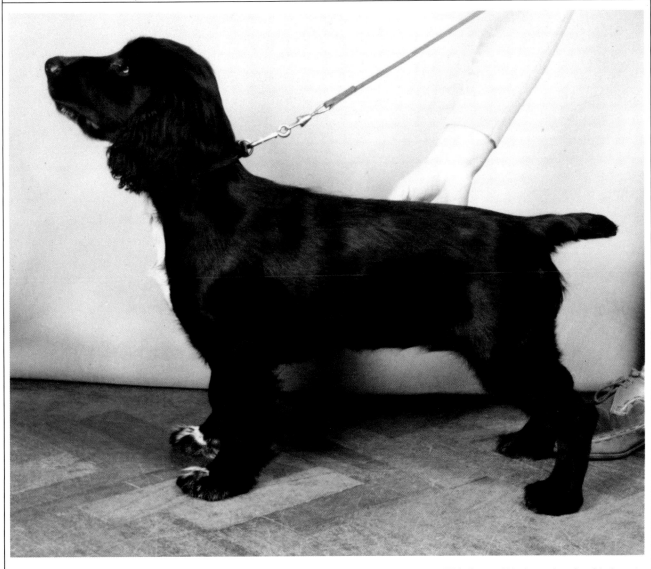

*Gundog group*

**Size**
Males and females: around 46 cm (18 ins) 16–23 kg (35–50.5 lbs)

**Coat**
Flat, or slightly waved. It should not be too short, and should never be curled. It is silky, glossy and refined. Although there is abundant feathering on the chest, under the belly and behind the legs, it should never be excessive.

**Colour**
The Field should be self coloured – black, red, liver, roan, or any of these with tan over the eyes, on the cheeks, feet and pasterns.

**Grooming**
The coat needs a good brush and comb a couple or so times a week for it to remain in good condition.

**Exercise**
This breed is built for activity and endurance. It needs plenty of exercise.

**Temperament**
Cheerful and reliable. Easy to manage and train.

**Suitability as a family companion**
This Spaniel's temperament and general bearing make it a good companion. It is level headed and intelligent and fits in well as a family dog, but it really does need exercise.

This is a well balanced and noble breed that combines beauty and utility. The noble head is quite a distinctive feature of this breed. The muzzle is long and lean. The eyes should not be too full, nor too small, receding or overhung. They should be dark hazel, brown or nearly black with a somewhat grave expression, showing no haw. The ears are well feathered, wide and moderately long, set low and falling in graceful folds. The lower parts curl inwards and backwards.

The chest is deep and well developed and the back and hindquarters should be muscular. The feet are round with good, strong pads. The tail is customarily docked and is carried low and well set on. As in all Spaniels, it is never carried above the level of the back.

# SPANIEL, IRISH WATER

*Gundog group*

**Size**
Males: 53–59 cm (21–23 ins)
Females: 51–56 cm (20–22 ins).

**Coat**
Dense tight crisp ringlets, free from
woolliness. The hair should have a
natural oiliness.

**Colour**
A rich dark liver with the purplish tint
or bloom peculiar to the breed. This
colour is sometimes referred to as
puce-liver.

**Grooming**
The tight curls do need a comb through
from time to time to keep them
tangle-free.

**Exercise**
This breed needs the chance to be active
and enjoy plenty of exercise.

**Temperament**
This breed does not mature quickly, but
retains many of its playful puppy traits
and high spirits until it is fully grown, at
around two years old. It is intelligent,
faithful and eager.

**Suitability as a family companion**
Its very even temperament and sense of
fun makes it an endearing companion.
It is easy to train.

This is the largest of the Spaniel family.
It is a versatile, adaptable and rugged
water dog.

The skull is long and high in dome,
covered with curls, to form a top-knot.
The nose, which is liver, is large and
well developed. The eyes should be
bright and alert, medium to dark
brown. The ears are very long.

The back is short and broad. The ribs
should have a large girth, making the
body barrel-shaped. The hindquarters
are powerful. The feet should be large,
round and somewhat spreading. The tail
should be short, straight, thick at the
root and tapering to a point. It should
be carried below the level of the back
line. The first seven to ten centimetres is
covered with close curls. The remainder
should be bare, or covered with fine,
straight hairs.

# SPANIEL, KING CHARLES

*Toy group*

**Size**
Males and females: ideally 3.6–6.3 kg
(8–14 lbs)

**Coat**
Long, silky and straight. A slight wave
is permitted, but it should not be curly.
The legs, ears and tail should be
profusely feathered.

**Colour**
Black-and-tan: a rich glossy black with
bright, mahogany-tan markings on legs,
chest, muzzle, the lining of the ears,
under the tail and a spot over eyes.
Tricolour: a ground colour of pearly
white and well distributed black patches
with brilliant tan markings on the
cheeks, the lining of the ears, under the
tail and as spots over the eyes. A wide
white blaze between the eyes.
Blenheim: a ground colour of pearly
white with well-distributed chestnut-red
patches and a wide clear white blaze,

with a clear red-chestnut spot in the
centre of the skull.
Ruby: a rich chestnut-red.

**Grooming**
It needs an occasional bath and a
regular brush and comb.

**Exercise**
It is not over-demanding. A garden, or
walk to the park is fine.

**Temperament**
It loves human companionship.

**Suitability as a family companion**
In the past, possibly because it was
more suited to a retired or regulated
household, the King Charles was
thought of as something for the
specialist owner. However, the breed
has taken on a new lease of life and is
well worth considering.

**Special needs**
Keep the eyes and ears clean.

The King Charles has an ancestry
similar to that of the Cavalier, but it is
more cobby and a little smaller, with a
shorter muzzle and low-set well
feathered ears. The two dogs existed
together, bearing the same name, for
several centuries, until the late 1920s.

In the King Charles, the head is most
important. It is massive, domed and has
a deep stop. The nose is black, with
large wide-open nostrils. The eyes are
very large and dark and set wide apart.
The tail is well feathered, and should
not be carried above the level of the
back. The movement is free, active and
elegant.

Those looking for a toy breed with a
difference might well be attracted by a
King Charles. It likes to be one of the
family: it is good with children and its
personality blossoms with tender loving
care.

# SPANIEL, SUSSEX

*Gundog group*

**Size**
Males: 38–41 cm (15–16 ins) 20.4 kg (45 lbs)
Females: 38–41 cm (15–16 ins) 18.2 kg (40 lbs)

**Coat**
Abundant and flat with no tendency to curl, with ample undercoat, giving good weather resistance.

**Colour**
Rich golden-liver with hair shading to gold at the tips, the gold predominating. A dark liver or puce is most objectionable.

**Grooming**
This dog needs a good brush and comb a couple or so times a week.

**Exercise**
This is an active working breed and likes plenty of exercise.

**Temperament**
Cheerful and tractable.

**Suitability as a family companion**
The Sussex is known best as a working Spaniel and, ideally, it should live in the country. Its temperament and devotion to its owner make it a good dog in the home.

The Sussex originated in the south of England. Its distinguishing feature is its colour: a lovely golden liver. The head is wide and moderately long and the skull has a slight curve from ear to ear. There should be a pronounced stop and frowning brows. The eyes are large, but not full and have a soft expression, with not much haw showing.

The ears are thick, fairly large and set low. The legs are rather short and moderately well feathered. The chest is deep and the whole body muscular, as are the thighs. The hindquarters should be well feathered above the hocks. The feet are well padded, round, and feathered between the toes. The tail is customarily docked. The dog has a decided and distinctive roll in its movement.

# SPANIEL, WELSH SPRINGER

*Gundog group*

**Size**
Males: 48 cm (19 ins)
Females: 46 cm (18 ins)

**Coat**
Straight or flat with a nice silky texture.
It should never be wiry, wavy or curly.

**Colour**
Rich red and white only.

**Grooming**
The richness of the coat colour and the
dog's well-being is enhanced by a
regular good brush and comb.

**Exercise**
This attractive breed needs a good
amount of exercise and the chance of a
free run.

**Temperament**
Sweet-natured, with an adaptable, even
disposition.

**Suitability as a family companion**
This is a loyal dog which is good with
children. It enjoys the company of both
humans and other animals and fits in
well into the home.

**Special needs**
It is easily bored and should not be left
alone for long periods.

This is an old pure breed which
originated in Wales. It is a good general
worker in all conditions and is a good
pupil. It enjoys its lessons, but it needs
to be started young.

It is symmetrical and compact: built
for endurance. The head is of medium
length with a slightly domed skull and a
clearly defined stop. The muzzle is
square, with well developed nostrils.
The eyes are hazel or dark and the ears
are set on low.

The body is strong and muscular and
the hindquarters are wide and well
developed. The feet are firm and cat-like
with thick pads. The tail is customarily
docked. It should be well set on and
low, never above the level of the back.
Movement should be quick and active,
showing plenty of push and drive.

# STAFFORDSHIRE BULL TERRIER

*Terrier group*

**Size**
Males: 35–40 cm (14–16 ins) 12.6–17 kg (28–38 lbs)
Females: 35–40 cm (14–16 ins) 10.8–15.3 kg (24–34 lbs)

**Coat**
Smooth, short and close to the skin.

**Colour**
Red, fawn, white, black or blue, or any of these colours with white. Any shade of brindle and white. Black-and-tan or liver colours are not encouraged.

**Grooming**
The Stafford requires little in the way of coat care to enhance its natural sheen. A regular brush and the occasional bath is all that is needed.

**Exercise**
This breed enjoys vigorous exercise.

**Temperament**
It is bold, but friendly. Its tough looks hide an intelligent nature. It can be aggressive with other dogs.

**Suitability as a family companion**
This is a good house guard and a real family dog: good with children and full of fun and mischief.

**Special needs**
Avoid confrontations with other dogs.

The Staffordshire Bull Terrier probably originated from Staffordshire, which was one of the last bastions of bull-baiting.

The dog is a medium-sized, powerful terrier. It is very strong for its size and is muscular, active and agile. The head is an important feature. It should have a broad skull, well developed cheek muscles, a pronounced stop and a strong, short foreface. The eyes should be dark, but may relate to the coat colour. They are round, and should look straight ahead. The ears should be rose, or half pricked, but not large.

The neck is muscular and short, the body short-coupled with a firm back and a wide front with plenty of heart and lung room. The hindquarters are well muscled, but relatively lighter. The tail is set low and tapers to a point.

The Staffordshire is a fine family dog which always aims to please. It respects firm handling.

# SWEDISH VALLHUND

*Working group*

**Size**
Males: 33 cm (13 ins) 9.9–14 kg (22–28 lbs)
Females: slightly shorter 9–10.5 kg (18–28 lbs)

**Coat**
The top coat is of medium length, harsh, close and well-fitting. The undercoat is abundant, soft and woolly.

**Colour**
Steel-grey or any shade of grey, reddish-brown or reddish-yellow with or without white markings, which must not exceed 30 per cent of the total colour.

**Grooming**
The easy-to-manage coat needs a regular brush and comb, more often when it is shedding.

**Exercise**
This is an energetic breed that will take and enjoy all the exercise it is given.

**Temperament**
This intelligent, adaptable dog enjoys life to the full.

**Suitability as a family companion**
This is a hardy, sensible-sized dog that is easily trained and quick to learn. It makes a good family pet and will be around for many years.

**Special needs**
It can be fond of the sound of its own voice. Be firm about controlling this, right from the beginning.

This breed was used in Sweden for centuries as a cattle dog. It had to be tough and energetic enough for all-day working, and it is set low to the ground to avoid kicks from the cattle. This is a sturdy dog, with an alert disposition.

It has a rather long head: clean-cut with an almost flat skull, well defined stop and a muzzle slightly shorter than the skull. The eyes are medium-sized, dark brown and oval. The expression is alert and bright, with upright, pointed ears. The neck should be long and strong.

The body is long with a level back and good strong bone and muscle. The movement should be smooth and purposeful. These dogs are often born without a tail: otherwise it should be docked.

The Swedish Vallhund is tough and adaptable. It is easy to look after and makes an attractive pet.

# WEIMARANER

*Gundog group*

**Size**
Males: 61–69 cm (24–27 ins)
Females: 56–64 cm (22–25 ins)

**Coat**
Short, smooth and sleek. There is a long-haired variety, in which the coat is usually 2.5–5 cm (1–2 inches) long on the body and somewhat longer on the neck, chest and belly. The tail and back of the limbs should be feathered.

**Colour**
Preferably shades of silver, mouse- or roe-grey, usually blending to a lighter shade on head and ears. The whole coat gives the appearance of a metallic sheen. A small white mark is permitted on the chest but nowhere else.

**Grooming**
A good rub over with the hound glove is usually enough.

**Exercise**
This is a hunting gundog of power and stamina. Its exercise needs reflect this.

**Temperament**
Fearless, friendly, protective and obedient. It learns its lessons early and well and is exceedingly trainable.

**Suitability as a family companion**
This is a versatile breed adaptable to many jobs. It is a good family dog and companion. Its clean lines and short coat make it easy to manage and clean about the house. It can appear somewhat cold and closely watchful of strangers, which can prove a good deterrent.

**Special needs**
This intelligent and responsive breed needs, and appreciates, firm handling for the best results.

The Weimaraner (pronounced *Vimeraner*) is sometimes called 'the grey ghost'. It was developed at the German court of Weimar and today it is widely regarded as an excellent all-round gundog.

It is an aristocratic, medium-sized breed, which should present a picture of grace, speed and balance. The head is fairly long, with a moderate stop. The jaw is powerful with quite deep flews. The eyes are medium-sized in shades of amber or blue-grey and have a keen and intelligent expression. The ears are set high and well back on the head.

The forequarters are straight and strong, and the body has a well developed chest. The hindquarters are muscular and the feet are firm and compact, with good pads. The tail is customarily docked. The movement should be effortless and smooth.

This is a striking, highly intelligent breed, whose appearance never fails to attract attention.

# WELSH CORGI, CARDIGAN

*Working group*

### Size
Males and females: 30 cm (12 ins) weight in proportion to size.

### Coat
Short or medium length, preferably straight of hard texture. Weatherproof, with a good undercoat.

### Colour
Any colour, including brindle and the attractive blue merle, all with or without white markings. White should not predominate.

### Grooming
There are no problems here. A good brush and comb is fine.

### Exercise
It enjoys exercise, and will take all that is given.

### Temperament
A steady, sensible dog.

### Suitability as a family companion
The handy-sized Cardigan is not an extrovert. It is devoted to its owner and is at home in either town or country.

This is one of the oldest of breeds. The Cardigan is generally a bigger dog than the Pembroke Corgi. The head is not quite as fine, while the ears are set wider apart. They are slightly rounder and somewhat larger in proportion to the size of the dog. It should have a foxy-looking head and an alert expression.

The chest is fairly broad, with a prominent breast-bone. There should be a clearly defined waist. The front legs are slightly bowed. The topline is level and the tail is fairly long and is set in line with the body. It is like a fox's brush, touching, or nearly touching the ground. The feet should be round, tight, well padded and rather large. The movement is free and active.

# WELSH CORGI, PEMBROKE

*Working group*

**Size**
Males: 25.4–30.4 cm (10–12 ins) 9–11 kg (20–24 lbs)
Females: 25.4–30.4 cm (10–12 ins) 8–10 kg (18–22 lbs)

**Coat**
Double coated of medium length, close lying, flat and dense. It should not be wiry.

**Colour**
Self colours in red, sable, fawn and black and tan or with white markings on legs, chest and neck. Some white on head and foreface is permissible. White should not predominate.

**Grooming**
This easy-to-manage coat needs little attention excepting a good regular brush or rub with a hound glove. It sheds twice a year.

**Exercise**
It enjoys walks and outings and is ideally suited to both town and country life.

**Temperament**
Faithful, intelligent and loyal.

**Suitability as a family companion**
The Corgi is a faithful family dog that loves to please. It is a good watch-dog and is easy to train.

The Corgi is a low-set, sturdy breed which is alert and active. It gives the impression of substance and stamina in a small space. It originated as a farm and drovers' dog in west Wales and for the past fifty years has been a favourite with the Royal family.

The head is foxy-looking, with erect, slightly pointed ears. The eyes are hazel, blending with the colour of the coat and are medium-sized, round and well set.

The dog should have good bone and the legs should be as short and straight as possible. The body is of medium length with well sprung ribs and a broad, deep chest. The tail is customarily docked.

This is a smart and attractive breed with a workmanlike structure. It is extremely popular as a family pet.

# WELSH TERRIER

*Terrier group*

**Size**
Males and females: 39 cm (15.5 ins) 9–9.5 kg (20–21 lbs)

**Coat**
Hard and wiry, very close and abundant. It should be a double coat – a single one is undesirable.

**Colour**
Black-and-tan, or black, grizzle-and-tan. It should be free from black pencillings on the toes. Black below the hocks is also a fault.

**Grooming**
It needs regular trimming of the harsh coat to keep it smart and attractive.

**Exercise**
It enjoys being active and likes regular walks.

**Temperament**
Game and fearless, but not pugnacious.

**Suitability as a family companion**
A first-class terrier in every way, it is ideally suited in size and robustness for both country and town life. It is intelligent and easily trained.

**Special needs**
A Welsh Terrier is normally hardy and robust in constitution and needs no pampering. It can be headstrong, so it needs firm but kind handling right form the first.

The Welsh Terrier is really only a variety of the old black-and-tan rough-haired terrier that has been developed in Wales for centuries.

The head should be flat and have strength and width between the ears. The jaws should be powerful and clean-cut. The ears are small, neat and 'V'-shaped. They are set on fairly high.

The front legs should be straight and muscular with good bone. The hindquarters should be strong with well bent hocks. The feet are small, round and cat-like. The tail is customarily docked. It should be well set on and carried high.

The handy-sized terrier has much in its favour as a town or country companion. It is second to none as a working terrier.

# WEST HIGHLAND WHITE TERRIER

*Terrier group*

**Size**
Males and females: 28 cm (11 ins)

**Coat**
Double-coated with a hard outercoat, free from any curl, and a short, soft undercoat.

**Colour**
Pure white.

**Grooming**
It needs regular combing as well as either a trim twice a year or regular plucking at its coat. It needs a bath from time to time. Do not be misled if you are told this is not good for the coat.

**Exercise**
It enjoys walks and romps in the park and is completely at home either in town or in the country.

**Temperament**
Full of self-esteem, lovable and faithful.

**Suitability as a family companion**
This dog is a good size. It is tough and has no fads about food. It is game for anything, loves human company and very easy to care for – all these attributes make it a popular family dog.

**Special needs**
It is important to keep its coat and nails in good order though the dog should not be pampered.

As its name implies, this dog originated in Scotland. It was used to go to ground in burrows.

The head is especially appealing – being thickly coated with hair so that it looks rather like a large white chrysanthemum. The dark, eyes and large black nose and small, neat, ears are combined with the cheeky expression that makes the 'Westie' hard to resist.

The body should be compact, with a level back. The tail is fairly short and is carried jauntily.

This tough, short-legged and lovable terrier looks very smart when kept well-groomed. It is a popular breed, which means you should take extra care about who you buy it from.

# WHIPPET

*Hound group*

**Size**
Males: 47 cm (18.5 ins)
Females: 44 cm (17.5 ins)

**Coat**
Fine, short.

**Colour**
Any colour or mixture of colours.

**Grooming**
The short coat presents no problems. Give the dog a regular rub down with the hound glove and an occasional spirit shampoo.

**Exercise**
The Whippet enjoys a run at liberty, and a small garden may not be enough. Regular walks will be essential.

**Temperament**
Affectionate, more timid than aggressive. It is not a fighter and not given to biting.

**Suitability as a family companion**
This is not a large dog. It is intelligent and obedient, and adapts easily to its home and surroundings. It makes a splendid, long-living family pet.

**Special needs**
Although a sporting dog, it should not be over exercised as a youngster.

The Whippet gives the impression of being beautifully balanced and powerful, with elegance and grace of outline. The head is long and lean, the ears small and fine in texture, the eyes bright, the expression alert.

The neck should be long and muscular, elegantly arched. The body has plenty of lung and heart room and a definite arch over the loin. The hindquarters should be strong and broad. The Whippet should possess great freedom of action. Its short coat and small feet make it exceptionally clean about the house.

This is an all-purpose dog, ideal for the sporting family. It is clean and although it may look delicate, it is exceptionally robust. It is well able to resist the elements and is rarely ill.

# YORKSHIRE TERRIER

*Toy group*

**Size**
Males and females: a maximum of 3.2 kg (7 lbs)

**Coat**
Moderately long, perfectly straight, of fine silky texture and glossy, like silk.

**Colour**
A dark steel-blue extends from the back of the skull to the roots of the tail. The hair on the chest, legs, head and face is a rich bright tan.

**Grooming**
This is a highly-groomed breed for the show ring. The coat does not moult and providing it is regularly brushed, combed and bathed, it should not present any problems to those who just have a Yorkie as a pet. The coat can easily be kept to a manageable length that is comfortable for the dog.

**Exercise**
This breed is ideal for those with limited accommodation or who cannot provide much exercise. Its needs are not great.

**Temperament**
Perky and game.

**Suitability as a family companion**
Hardy and alert, the Yorkshire Terrier makes a good watchdog. It is very protective of its family and home.

This little dog originated in the mining communities of Yorkshire as a terrier-type dog for underground hunting.

The long coat is parted down the centre from the nose to the end of the tail, so that it hangs evenly on each side. The hair on the head is gathered up and is usually tied with a bow or a clip.

The hair on the muzzle is a rich, golden tan. The tan on the head should not extend to the neck, and no dark hair should mingle with the tan. The eyes are dark and sparkling. They look directly forward. The ears are 'V'-shaped and are carried erect.

The front legs are well covered with rich tan hair which does not extend higher than the elbows. The hindquarters are strong and the hair on the hindlegs is also a rich tan.

The tail is carried a little higher than the back and is customarily docked.